BLACK WITNESS TO THE APOSTOLIC FAITH

Edited by

DAVID T. SHANNON
and
GAYRAUD S. WILMORE

WILLIAM B. EERDMANS PUBLISHING COMPANY
GRAND RAPIDS, MICHIGAN
FOR
COMMISSION ON FAITH AND ORDER
NATIONAL COUNCIL OF THE CHURCHES OF CHRIST
IN THE U.S.A.

This edition first published 1988 for the Commission on Faith and Order,
NCCCUSA, 475 Riverside Dr., Room 872, New York, NY 10115-0050
(212) 870-2569,
by Wm. B. Eerdmans Publishing Co., 255 Jefferson Ave. SE,
Grand Rapids, Mich. 49503

These materials, except the Introduction, were originally published in
Mid-Stream: An Ecumenical Journal, vol. XXIV, no. 4, October 1985,
edited by Paul A. Crow, Jr.
The Commission on Faith and Order and the publisher wish to express their
appreciation to *Mid-Stream* for permission to reprint these materials and to
acknowledge the assistance of the Commission staff in producing this volume:
    Brother Jeffrey Gros, director
    Stefanie Yova Yazge
    Carol Thysell
    Barbara Henninges

CONTENTS

INTRODUCTION

The articles and documents contained in this volume represent a few of the most recent contributions by African American Christians in the United States to the World Council of Churches' continuing discussion of the nature of the apostolic faith around the world today and how that faith should be confessed both universally and in particular situations. This material has also been useful as a resource for theological work on the same issues in the Commission on Faith and Order of the National Council of Churches of Christ in the United States (NCCCUSA). As coeditors we are pleased to join the Commission on Faith and Order in thanking *Mid-Stream* for permission to reprint this study. We wish also to express our special appreciation to Brother Jeffrey Gros, F.S.C., the indefatigable director of the Commission, for his good offices and hard work in making this study by black American theologians and church leaders more widely known and available.

This book, and the one building upon it,[1] are the first two in a new series of NCCC Faith and Order studies to be published by William B. Eerdmans Publishing Company. In addition to the volumes in this series, Faith and Order has made available a study guide on the Nicene Creed,[2] two studies on the Holy Spirit,[3] and one on Christology.[4] The Commission on Faith and Order has linked the study of the Pentecostal churches with the black church study because of the historic significance of both African American and Hispanic church development in the emergence and phenomenal growth of Pentecostalism in the twentieth century. This particular volume, therefore, should not be studied in isolation from either present or future studies by the NCCCUSA, or from the wider range of bilateral and multilateral investigations seeking to unite the divided churches.[5] It is important for the reader to re-

---

1. Thaddeus D. Horgan, ed., *Apostolic Faith in America* (Grand Rapids: Eerdmans, 1988).

2. *Confessing One Faith: Grounds for a Common Witness. A Guide for Ecumenical Study* (Cincinnati: Forward Movement Publications, 1988).

3. Mark Heim and Theodore Stylianopolos, eds., *The Spirit of Truth* (Brookline, Mass.: Holy Cross Press, 1986); "Confessing the Apostolic Faith from the Perspective of the Pentecostal Churches," *Pneuma* 9:1 (spring 1987).

4. Paul Fries and Tiran Nersoyan, *Christ in East and West* (Macon, Ga.: Mercer University Press, 1987).

5. See Lukas Vischer and Harding Meyer, *Growth in Agreement: Reports and*

gard this book as an essential part of the whole corpus of Faith and
Order studies in process both in the United States and around the
world.[6]

This is especially desirable in view of the subordinate status
and marginal role that the ecumenical movement has previously
assigned to theological work done by Africans and African Americans in North America, South America, and the Caribbean. Although Dr. Benjamin Elijah Mays, a distinguished black delegate
to the First Assembly of the World Council of Churches in 1948,
said he found no racial segregation or discrimination in Amsterdam,[7] it must be noted that neither at Amsterdam in 1948 nor at
subsequent meetings of units of the World Council of Churches—
with the possible exception of the Programme to Combat Racism—
has the theological work of Christians in Africa and the diaspora
received sufficient and serious attention.

Of course, it has always been true that "he who pays the piper
calls the tune" and that the white churches of Europe and North
America have contributed the greatest moral and financial support
to the World Council of Churches and the NCCC. But that is as it
should be. The debt of centuries of black exploitation is not yet
fully paid. For five hundred years the white churches of the West
have enjoyed the material benefits of the systematic extortion of
the brains, brawn, and natural resources of the two-thirds world
that is nonwhite. It cannot be claimed that the Christian churches
have had nothing to do with this lamentable reality. The "Christian
civilization" they helped to implant among those nonwhite people
has certainly not been an unmixed blessing. In the United States,
at least, African American Christians have struggled for more than
two centuries to reinterpret and revise a distorted gospel that we
received from white Christians who held us in bondage for almost

Agreed Statements of Ecumenical Conversations on a World Level (New York: Paulist,
1984); Jeffrey Gros and Joseph Burgess, eds., *Building Unity* (New York: Paulist, 1988);
and J. F. Puglisi and S. J. Voicu, eds., *A Bibliography of Interchurch and Interconfessional Theological Dialogues* (Rome: Centro Pro Unione, 1984).

6. See the WCC publications *Confessing One Faith: Toward an Ecumenical Explication of the Apostolic Faith as Expressed in the Nicene- Constantinopolitan Creed
(381),* Study Document, Faith and Order Paper No. 140 (Geneva: World Council of
Churches, 1987); and Thomas Best, ed., *Faith and Renewal: Commission on Faith and
Order, Stravanger, 1985* (Geneva: World Council of Churches, 1986). Gayraud Wilmore
headed the subsection on "Problems of Recognition of the Apostolic Faith in the Nicene
Creed and Areas for Common Confession / Expression Today," pp. 157-65, where some
of these issues were discussed.

7. Benjamin E. Mays, *Born to Rebel: An Autobiography* (Athens, Ga.: University
of Georgia Press, 1987), p. 254.

two hundred fifty years and who then subjected us to one of the most degrading forms of racial segregation and discrimination that the world has ever known. The member churches of the World Council, the Roman Catholic Church, and other major denominations in Europe and North America might be obliged for some time to come to adopt compensatory policies and procedures to repair justly the injuries that blacks and other nonwhite ethnic groups have suffered as a consequence of slavery, colonialism, neo-colonialism, classism, and racism, officially and unofficially aided and abetted by Western Christianity.

The First Assembly of the WCC in 1948 was an auspicious beginning for a kind of corrective ecumenism unprecedented in the modern world. In the message from Amsterdam the word went out:

> Our coming together to form a World Council will be vain unless Christians and Christian congregations everywhere commit themselves to the Lord of the Church in a new effort to seek together, where they live, to be His witnesses and servants among their neighbors. We have to remind ourselves and all men that God has put down the mighty from their seats and exalted the humble and meek. We have to learn afresh together and speak boldly in Christ's name both to those in power and to the people, to oppose terror, cruelty and race discrimination, to stand by the outcast, the prisoner and the refugee.[8]

The World Council of Churches, lest we forget, began with a solid commitment to racial justice as an indispensable requirement of the Christian unity it sought. More than twenty black Americans shared the promise of a new ecumenical agency that would rid the churches of the sin of racism by participating in the discussions that produced the reports of the First Assembly. Among them were such notable church leaders and theologians as the African Methodist Episcopal Zion Bishop William J. Walls; the Colored Methodist Episcopal Bishop A. J. Bishop; Dr. William H. Jernagin, pastor of the Mt. Carmel Baptist Church of Washington, D.C.; Dr. J. H. Jackson, pastor of the famous Olivet Baptist Church of Chicago; A.M.E. Bishop S. L. Greene, who was also a member of the Commission on Faith and Order; Bishop D. Ward Nichols of the A.M.E. Church; and the president of Morehouse College in Atlanta, Dr. Benjamin E. Hays. Also in attendance as accredited visitors, youth delegates, or consultants were Mrs. Albie E. C.

8. *The Universal Church in God's Design: An Ecumenical Study Prepared under the Auspices of the World Council of Churches* (London: SCM, 1948), p. 208.

Jackson, the executive secretary of the A.M.E. Zion Women's Home and Foreign Mission Society; Philip Potter of Jamaica, then a ministerial student in England; and Rena Karefa-Smart of the A.M.E. Zion Church, who was living at the time in Sierra Leone. We were not lacking in either mature or budding theologians at Amsterdam!

In this year 1988 we do well to celebrate the fortieth anniversary of the birth of the WCC with the publication of this slim volume on one small part of the African American contribution to the contemporary ecumenical movement. But our purpose in these pages is not to celebrate the past as much as to remind our brothers and sisters in Christ that the future of church unity may well depend upon the reappropriation of the spirit and intent of Amsterdam concerning deeds over words, visible fulfillment over specious promises, in the encounter between church and race.

One of the problems we see with Faith and Order today, whether in Geneva or New York, is that too many theological discussions and studies neglect the fact that we are not called to love in word and in speech, but in deed and in truth (1 John 3:18). No amount of profound theologizing about the necessity of the Nicene Creed or the coherence of Baptism, Eucharist, and Ministry will please God nearly as much as loosening the bonds of wickedness in the church, letting the oppressed go free, and breaking every yoke (Isaiah 58:6). This does not mean that black theologians in the United States are indifferent about devoting much theological work and energy toward the goal of Christian unity. It does mean, however, that we have frequently found that ponderous theological debates and documents are used as substitutes for action, for doing something specific about a problem, for making demands upon heretical congregations, for allocating those human, material, and financial resources that can make for greater equality, justice, and love in the household of faith.

Let us not mistake ecclesiology for a converted heart and made-up mind. Obsession with the subtleties of dialectics and dogmatics must not be permitted to blind us or our people to what the Lord requires of the churches in a world of enormous human suffering and need. On this fortieth anniversary of the First Assembly of the World Council, we call ourselves and others back to the spirit and commitment of Amsterdam. We remind ourselves and others of the words of the Report on Section I on the Universal Church in God's Design:

> Within our divided churches it is to our shame that we have so often lived in preoccupation with our internal affairs, looking inward upon

our own concerns instead of forgetting ourselves in outgoing love and service. Our churches are too much dominated by ecclesiastic officialdom, clerical or lay, instead of giving vigorous expression to the full rights of the living congregation and the sharing of clergy and people in the common life in the Body of Christ. *We pray for the churches' renewal as we pray for their unity. As Christ purifies us by His Spirit we shall find that we are drawn together and that there is no gain in unity unless it is unity in truth and holiness.*[9]

GAYRAUD WILMORE AND DAVID SHANNON

9. *The Universal Church in God's Design,* p. 216.

BLACK WITNESS TO THE APOSTOLIC FAITH

JEFFREY GROS

The Faith and Order movement is indebted to Dr. Gayraud Wilmore, Dean, New York Theological Seminary and Dr. David Shannon, President, Virginia Union University, for focusing discussion among the Black Churches on the World and National Councils' study, "Towards the Common Expression of the Apostolic Faith Today". A special consultation was held on December 14 and 15, 1984 at Virginia Union University, Richmond, Virginia, reporting to the National Council Commission plenary on March 22, 1985 in Atlanta. Scholars from twelve different churches drafted the statement "Toward a Common Expression of Faith: A Black North American Perspective" for presentation to the World Council Commission at its plenary in Stavanger, Norway in August 1985 as well as to the National Council Apostolic Faith Study.

The working paper by Gayraud Wilmore, "Black Christians, Church Unity and One Common Expression of Apostolic Faith" (see p. 357ff), circulated in preparation for the consultation proposed the Black Church Consultation as part of the larger Apostolic Faith Study, which is an attempt to provide the churches with an understanding of the biblical faith, explicated in the contemporary context of the churches, that can serve as a basis for church union.[1] The World Council will have completed four consultations on the theme in preparation for the Stavanger meeting, centering on Faith, Christ, the Holy Spirit and God the Creator. The National Council, which has been at work on this study for only three years, has completed five consultations in addition to the one recorded in this volume: Creeds and the Churches, Language and the Creeds, Scripture and Creeds, the Apostolic Faith in Relationship to the Jewish Faith, and Christology.[2] Subsequent United States consultations are planned on the doctrine of the Holy Spirit,

Brother Jeffrey Gros, F.S.C. served as Director of the Commission on Faith and Order of the National Council of Churches of Christ in the USA.

1. Michael Kinnamon, ed., *Towards Visible Unity*, Volumes I and II, Faith and Order Papers No. 112, 113 (Geneva: World Council of Churches, 1982); Faith and Order Paper No. 121, Minutes, Standing Commission of Faith and order, Crete, (Geneva: World Council of Churches, 1984); Hans-Georg Link, ed., *The Roots of Our Common Faith: Faith in the Scriptures and in the Early Church*, (Geneva, World Council of Churches, 1984).

2. Paulos Gregorios, William Lazareth and Nikos Nissiotis, eds., *Does Chalcedon Divide or Unite? Towards Convergence in Orthodox Christology* (Geneva: World Council of Churches, 1981); Mark Heim, "Gender and Creed: Confessing a Common Faith", *Christian Century*, p. 379, 4/17/85; *Union Seminary Quarterly Review*, Volume 40, #3, August 1985. (Special Issue on Language and the Creeds).

The Apostolic Faith from the perspective of Pentecostal Churches, and the meaning of Apostolic Faith in the context of the U. S. churches.

It is hoped that by the 1988 World Conference on Faith and Order, a document may be produced for study in the churches comparable to the document "Baptism, Eucharist and a Mutually Recognized Ministry" produced by the World Council Commission at its 1974 meeting in Accra.[3] This project of both synthesizing the multiplicity of confessions with their rich diversity,[4] and specifying the essential basis for common confession, relies heavily on dialogues going on elsewhere in the Faith and Order movement; in bilateral dialogues,[5] church union negotiations,[6] and individual proposals by theologians of stature.[7] The work of the theologians contributing to this study is an important infusion of life into this dialogue on the doctrinal basis for a restored unity in the body of Christ.

At Nairobi, 1975, the World Council put before the world a vision for the unity of the Church, in each place and in all places, that would consist of a Conciliar Fellowship of churches, following the model of Acts 15 and the early ecumenical councils.[8] The National Council Commission has undertaken a similar study and returned a report to the World Council Commission. Both of these studies look upon at least three elements as necessary before a General Council of the Church, worldwide, Protestant, Orthodox and Catholic, could be called again: agreement on 1) Baptism, Eucharist and Ordained Ministry; 2) The common faith as handed

3. *One Baptism, One Eucharist and a Mutually Recognized Ministry*, Faith and Order Paper No. 73, (Geneva: World Council of Churches, 1975); *Towards an Ecumenical Consensus on Baptism, Eucharist and Ministry*, Faith and Order Paper No. 84 (Geneva: World Council of Churches, 1977).

4. Hans-Georg Link, ed., *Confessing Our Faith Around the World*, Volume I (Faith and Order Paper No. 104, 1980), Volume II, (Faith and Order Paper No. 120, 1983), Volume III, (Faith and Order Paper No. 123, 1984) [all Geneva: World Council of Churches].

5. Harding Meyer and Lukas Vischer, eds., *Growth in Agreement*, Faith and Order Paper No. 108, (New York: Paulist Press, 1984).

6. *Growing Towards Consensus and Commitment*, Faith and Order Paper No. 110, (Geneva: World Council of Churches, 1981); Gerald Moede, ed., *The COCU Consensus: In Quest of a Church of Christ Uniting*, (Princeton, NJ: COCU, 1985); *Fourth Forum on Bilateral Conversations*: Report, Faith and Order Paper No. 125, (Geneva: World Council of Churches, 1985); *Midstream* Vol. XXIII, No. 3, July 1984.

7. George Lindbeck, *The Nature of Doctrine: Religion and Theology in a Postliberal Age*, (Philadelphia: Westminster Press, 1984); Heinrich Fries and Karl Rahner, *The Unity of the Churches: An Actual Possibility*, (New York: Philadelphia: Fortress/Paulist Presses, 1985).

8. David Paton, ed., *Breaking Barriers,* Nairobi 1975 (London: SPCK and Grand Rapids: Wm. B. Eerdmans, 1976); *The Ecumenical Review* Vol. XXVI No. 2, (April 1974).

on from the Apostles; 3) ways of deciding and acting together. The 1982 statement on *Baptism, Eucharist and Ministry* of the World Council Commission is a major contribution towards fulfilling the first basis, should it find serious reception in the churches.[9] The study to which this consultation is a contribution, "Towards the Common Expression of the Apostolic Faith Today", is designed to produce a basis in faith to which the churches can respond on the pilgrimage to a confession of the faith in common.

Of course, the presence of the Black Church voices are not new to the ecumenical movement, as Wilmore indicates.[10] In National Council work, however, they are often muted in the debates among historic Protestant traditions as well as between these traditions and Orthodox and Roman Catholic voices. The National Council, in its presentation of the Conciliar Fellowship vision for the U.S. context, has been careful to include a fourth note: "Ending Prejudices and Hostilities", as its first premise on which unity must be based.[11] This study emphasizes reconciliation among races, sexes and classes as central to the project of Christian unity: "A people proposing reconciliation among all women and men while not earnestly seeking reconciliation and unity between all Christians will increasingly be a scandal and spectacle to the world."[12] In the National Council study there is a clear confession that we have lengths to go to realize this evangelical reconciliation:

> Only cynics would deny the gains made in transcending divisions of confession, race, and sex in many of our relationships as American Christians in recent years. The gains, however, because of their modesty and their human cost, impel us to recognize two things: that we have much farther to go, but also that we have enough positive experiences amidst our heterogeneity to be more confident about the future.[13]

In the World Council study, *Baptism, Eucharist and Ministry*, the churches are called upon to recognize the integral character of Eucharistic life and ethical life, building a Body of Christ that transcends the human and sinful divisions we bring to the table:

---

9. Jeffrey Gros, ed., *The Search for Visible Unity*, (New York: Pilgrim Press, 1984); *Baptism, Eucharist and Ministry*, Faith and Order Paper No. 111, (Geneva: World Council of Churches, 1982); Fr. Max Thurian and Geoffrey Wainwright, eds., *Baptism and Eucharist: Ecumenical Convergence in Celebration*, (Geneva: World Council of Churches, 1983); Jeffrey Gros, "Baptism, Eucharist and Ministry" *One World*, January 1985.

10. Gayraud Wilmore, James Cone, eds., *Black Theology: A Documentary History, 1966-1979*, (Maryknoll, NY: Orbis Books, 1979).

11. "Conciliar Fellowship", p. 252, *Midstream* Vol. XXI, No. 2, (April 1982).

12. *Ibid.*, p. 255.

13. *Ibid.*, p. 266.

> As participants in the eucharist, therefore, we prove inconsistent if we are not actively participating in this ongoing restoration of the world's situation and the human condition . . . All kinds of injustice, racism, separation and lack of freedom are radically challenged when we share in the body and blood of Christ. Through the eucharist the all-renewing grace of God penetrates and restores human personality and dignity.[14]

It is hoped that this consultation, the fine papers it produced and the final report, "Toward a Common Expression of Faith: A Black North American Perspective", will make possible such care and sensitivity in the drafting and understanding of the final statement to be put before the churches from the Apostolic Faith studies of the World and National Councils of Churches' Faith and Order Commissions.

The four papers prepared in response to Dr. Wilmore's initial treatment of the topic provide a wide array of perspectives and issues which helped the participants in the conference surface the themes included in their statement. In addition to the four Protestant papers, which included one from the Church of God in Christ, a paper from a major Pentecostal communion not yet a member of either of the Councils, the recent pastoral letter from the Black Roman Catholic bishops was circulated prior to the consultation. Roman Catholic theologians, who had planned to attend were unable to do so, so the statement does not include their input. For that reason we have included "What We Have Seen and Heard" as a Catholic contribution to this issue. Hopefully, this Apostolic Faith study will provide an opportunity for dialogue and common Black witness across Catholic and Protestant lines. Several Black Catholic theologians and bishops have been involved in the discussions throughout the process.

This consultation is particularly dedicated to the memory and work of Dr. W. Jerry Boney, who served for sixteen years on the faculty of Virginia Union University, and for thirteen months as the Director of the Faith and Order Commission of the National Council of Churches. His life was devoted to the reconciling ministry of black and white, Catholic, Orthodox, and Protestant, and of all elements of the Christian life that found themselves divided from one another.

Finally, Faith and Order hopes that this volume will provide the opportunity for local study within the Black community, among Christians of a variety of traditions and races and in parts of the world where the witness of the Black churches is not personally present. The presence of the Black Pentecostal voices and the contact with Roman Catholic scholars lifts up a sign to the

---

14. *Baptism, Eucharist and Ministry*, "Eucharist", D. #20.

wider ecumenical movement, which the Councils seek to serve as they seek to "call the churches to the goal of visible unity in one faith and in one Eucharistic fellowship expressed in worship and in common life in Christ, and to advance towards that unity in order that the world may believe."

TOWARD A COMMON EXPRESSION OF FAITH: A BLACK NORTH AMERICAN PERSPECTIVE

DAVID T. SHANNON

The purpose of this brief paper is to give an introduction to the work of our task force which addressed the common expression of the apostolic faith from the perspective of Black Christians in the United States. The details of the report are provided by Dr. Gayraud Wilmore, co-chairperson of this task force. The focus of this introduction is stress on at least three parallels between the formulation of the apostolic creed and the Black experience in America. First there is a contextual parallel. Both the persons who formulated creeds and the slaves who formed the Black religious experience came out of oppression. Those who exclaimed "I believe in God Almighty" had mud on their sandals from the catacombs.

From The Catacombs To Confession.

The study and reflection upon the background of the creed, especially the Nicene creed carries us back to Nicaea in A.D. 325. This historical date reminds us that the church was emerging from political oppression which forced them to endure hardship and violent persecution. They were called atheist; their status was that of illegal worshipers of a false God until Constantine gave official recognition to them in the edit of Milan in 318. Their precarious position led them to flee to the catacombs—underground tunnels/caves for worship, teaching and mutual support. One early writer observed: "The blood of the martyrs became the seed of the church." The catacombs were their sanctuary as they readied themselves to face the lions in the amphitheaters for the enjoyment of the kings and Roman citizens. They came to the council from their experience of the catacombs. They came to confess their faith in God. They celebrated the mighty acts of God as they moved from experience to confession, from praxis to doxa.

This movement from the context of oppression to confession is the story of the Black American's experience in this country. The Black American experience in America, their being uprooted from Africa, their enslavement in this country—their ontological denial, their existential rejection and their toils, struggles and horrors in the North American continent—could have led them to despair, and rejection of Christianity. But like their Christian forebears,

___
Dr. Shannon serves as Academic Dean and Professor of Old Testament at the Interdenominational Theological Seminary in Atlanta, Georgia.

6

they moved from oppression to confession. Whereas the formulators of the creed came from the catacombs, the formers of religion among Black Americans came from the underground railroad, the slave huts and toil in the midday sun. From sun up to sun down they labored, but from sun down to sun up they forged their faith.

The second parallel is that they moved from practice to confession, from praxis to doxa.

From Praxis To Doxa

One of the curious omissions of the early creeds is their lack of emphasis upon practice-*praxis*. The emphasis is upon doctrine—belief concerning God, Jesus Christ, the church, eternal life. This omission on praxis is due to the fact that those who formulated the creed brought the praxis in their person. Like Paul they bore the stigmata of Christ on their bodies. Like him they could say "I bare in my body the marks (stigmata) of Christ". Their biographies were the practice, the praxis.

Likewise, the Black Christian came to confession from praxis, practice. Slavery forced the slaves to experience God before reflection upon him. This paradigm comes out of the Old and New Testament experience. They encountered God in their history. Later, they reflected upon His Mighty Acts and have left us their legacy in the Bible.

Emphasis upon this order of the relationship between praise and faith is informative as we focus upon the meaning of the apostolic faith today. We must reaffirm the necessary symbiosis between praxis and doxa, not the reverse. One of the concerns has been the failure to follow the models from the Old Testament, the New Testament, the Apostolic Age—the stress on doing theology before abstracting theology.

Yet we affirm that there is a tension—a necessary tension—between the two. Praxis without doxa is humanism; doxa without praxis is theosophy.

The Next Parallel is that they Celebrated the Mighty Act of God in Jesus Christ—What a Mighty God

Both the formulators of the creeds and the bards who forged the Black religion in America began with the affirmation of God as the Mighty One. Although the lines in the creed give more detail to the birth, suffering death and resurrection of Jesus the Christ, the role of Christ is seen as a historical demonstration of God as the Mighty One, the Creator. Christ is the affirmation of God's continuing power as Creator. The Almighty One comes in Christ the creator. The Almighty One comes in Christ to create a new world, a new humanity. This sense of God the Creator who comes in Jesus the Christ who is the one who has the whole world in his hands.

He's got the whole world in his hands,
He's got the whole world in his hands,
He's got the whole world in his hands,
He's got the whole world in his hands.

He's got the little bitty baby in his hands,
He's got the little bitty baby in his hands,
He's got the little bitty baby in his hands,
He's got the whole world in his hands.

He's got you and me in his hands,
He's got you and me in his hands,
He's got you and me in his hands,
He's got the whole world in his hands.

He's got the wind and the rain in his hands,
He's got the wind and the rain in his hands,
He's got the wind and the rain in his hands,
He's got the whole world in his hands.

BLACK CHRISTIANS, CHURCH UNITY AND ONE COMMON EXPRESSION OF APOSTOLIC FAITH

GAYRAUD S. WILMORE

Almost twenty million Christians in the United States are concentrated in seven historic Black and in eight or nine predominantly white denominations, including the Roman Catholic church. These Afro-American Christians, even those in the white denominations who comprise less than twenty percent of the total, have maintained a relative independence and experienced relative isolation from the majority since the Civil War.

An attenuated but continuing nexus to an African past has stamped a distinctive mood and mode upon the spirituality, music and forms of worship of this segment of American Christians. A common participation in what was originally a blend of diasporic African culture with a culture of poverty in rural slums and urban ghettos has given these Black Christians an awareness of mutual lifestyles and group identity. An experience of racial prejudice and oppression has given them a sense of solidarity in suffering and struggle for more than 375 years.

These characteristics and others have convinced many scholars that it is accurate to speak of a Black or Afro-American Church in North America, even though there may be considerable diversity among its constituent parts. The trend toward racial integration in American society in the 20th century has only slightly dissolved this apparently unmeltable ethnic institution. It continues to grow, particularly among Pentecostal, Baptist, Methodist and Roman Catholic groups, and wields a disproportionate influence in the social, political and religious life of the nation. As far as Protestantism is concerned, the Black Church is now its principal representative in more than a score of the largest central cities in the United States.

It should come, therefore, as no surprise that the World Council of Churches and other ecumenical bodies are interested in what the Black Church believes and is prepared to commit to the movement toward visible unity. Accordingly, the Commission on Faith and Order of the National Council of Churches, in response to initiatives from Geneva, has undertaken to encourage Black theologians and church leaders to articulate the ideas and beliefs that seem generally to be approved and shared by Black churches, including those continuing to exist within predominantly white

Dr. Wilmore is Professor of Afro-American Religious Studies at the Interdenominational Theological Seminary in Atlanta, Georgia.

denominations. To what extent do Black Christians hold the same faith professed by other Christians in the United States and in other parts of the world? To what extent do they believe and practice a variant faith which is, nevertheless, rooted and grounded in the Apostolic tradition, as far as anyone can reconstruct that tradition today? What distinctive contributions do the Afro-American churches have to make to the quest, that has been accelerating since the founding of the WCC in 1948, for the visible unity of the one, holy, catholic and apostolic Church and the one expression of the faith handed down from Jesus and the apostles?

The purpose of this working paper is to discuss briefly some of the factors that may shape the appropriate context for addressing such questions. What follows below has no status except as a stimulus for an exploratory conversation at the Interchurch Center on May 30, 1984 and further discussion at a national conference in December. It is hoped that some of the problems and issues lifted up herein will be more thoroughly explored at the larger consultation now scheduled for December 14, 15 at Virginia Union University, Richmond, VA.

I. CHRISTIANITY AND RACISM

In 1975 the writer moderated a WCC consultation in Europe on ''Racism in Theology and Theology Against Racism''. The second chapter of the consultation report was published in a compendium of *WCC Statements and Actions on Racism, 1948-79*, edited by Ans J. van der Bent, (Geneva, 1980). Why was the first chapter on ''Racism in Theology'' eliminated from the official collection of policy statements? Was it because it contained one of the most devastating criticisms of Christianity ever issued by an international conference of Christian theologians and social scientists? This part of the document that the WCC has neglected to publicize analyzes Christian history and declares in no uncertain terms that theology has been infected by the ideology of white racism almost from its beginning. From the infiltration into the medieval church of the disparaging account of the origin of the physiognomy of African people—first promulgated by the Babylonian Talmud of the 6th century, A.D. to the modern defense of the subjugation and enslavement of Black people by some theologians of the American churches prior to 1861, Western Christendom, with few exceptions has been corrupted by a more vicious form of racism than was ever known in the pagan world.

If racism, as George Kelsey has so effectively argued, is diametrically opposite to a Christian understanding of creation and redemption, one might ask if Euro-American Christianity was totally corrupted—particularly in its Anglo-Saxon versions—by a deep-seated antipathy to Blackness. Certainly many Black Christians have thought so. For years some of our best thinkers and writers have expressed the opinion that what most white people believed and practiced as their religion could never be properly called Christianity. Thus, the Rev. W. Paul Quinn of the AME Church wrote in 1834 words that have echoed from Black pulpits for almost two hundred years:

> Can anything be a greater mockery of religion than the way in which it is conducted by the Americans? It appears as though they are bent only on daring God Almighty to do his best—they chain and handcuff us and go into the house of the God of justice to return Him thanks for having aided them in the infernal cruelties inflicted upon us. . . Will He not stop them, preachers and all? (Dorothy Porter, *Early Negro Writing*, Beacon, p. 630).

Some have held that the faith once delivered to the Apostles could only be found in the church that practiced and defended slavery if those churches experienced true repentance and total reformation. To the extent that the churches of Europe were participants or silent partners in the enslavement and subsequent oppression of Blacks and other non-white peoples, it was argued that they too needed to demonstrate genuine repentance and love in *koinonia* with the oppressed before their profession of the Christian faith could be taken seriously.

All this is only to say that Black Christians, for the most part, have never taken for granted that the Apostolic Faith, being invoked by the World Council of Churches these days, is resident in the white churches of Europe and North America—Protestant or Roman Catholic. This is not to say that Blacks have been correct in this judgment, but only to make a statement of fact. It does appear, however, that mere assent to the Nicene Creed and adherence to the great confessions of the Reformation does not, by itself, add up to apostolicity. As those of us who supported the Black Manifesto contended in 1969, many white churches—both in the U.S. and abroad—are still enjoying prosperity and wealth accumulated from the ill-gotten gain of the Atlantic slave trade. Until there is among such churches "fruit meet for repentance", African and Afro-American Christians may feel justified in looking elsewhere for signs of the unbroken continuity of pure religion from the Apostles to the present. It seems fair to ask whether at some time during the last millenium the message of Jesus and the New Testament all but evaporated from the Euro-American Church and society because of the gross incompatibility between faith and practice among those who called themselves Christians.

II. BLACK THEOLOGY AS APOLOGIA AND CRITIQUE

Black theology, from George Liele and David George to James Cone, has been an apologia for Black belief in the justice and righteousness of God and, usually by implication and indirection, a critique of an apostate white Church. This does not mean that Black thinkers did not appreciate the theological symbols of white Christendom—such as the Apostles Creed and the Shorter Catechism. Indeed the Black Church used them and extrapolated their truths for our own Disciplines and statements of faith. Most of the Blackness or "ethnic-specific content" in our theology has been in defense of the way we perceived God and worshiped him, an exhortation to Blacks to be more faithful to the Gospel than their masters and mistresses, or a protest against the abuses and injustices of the white Church, the white-dominated State and the social institutions of the nation. The fact that most of this Black content was never written down in books or ensconced in creeds and confessions does not make it any the less theological.

Nevertheless, any project that seeks to explicate what perceptions of Black Christians might be salvageable for a contemporary ecumenical statement of the Christian faith should, first of all, consider the writings, addresses and sermons of Black preachers, church leaders, theologians and philosophers—from Prince Hall and Henry M. Turner to W.E.B. DuBois and Cornell West. Secondly, the folklore, proverbs, spirituals, hymns and gospel songs are indispensable resources for understanding the belief structures of poor people who considered themselves just as much in succession to the Apostles and Fathers of the early Church as white folks. Some Black preachers assumed that the mantle of authority had actually fallen from the white churches to land upon the shoulders of Black believers, many of whom were slaves and illiterate. It was they who reconstructed an authentic faith from the compromised religion of the white man. The influence of this Black folk religion still reverberates in our churches, particularly in the Baptist, Methodist and Holiness-Pentecostal traditions. Any consideration, therefore, of Black theology that fails to include this data will be unable to identify the strands of the popular religion that may not have been woven into the official theologies of the churches but are essential for understanding the operative theology of the people.

The point of these remarks about Black theology is to suggest that although Black and white Christians received what is basically the same inheritance of the Gospel they have differed from one another in the emphasis, articulation and nuances of interpretation given both to Scripture and tradition. This fact, which some of us almost take for granted, seems difficult for Christians outside of the United States to understand. Often participants in international theological conferences want to brush it aside. Twenty years ago they may have been intrigued by unfamiliar theological ideas exploding from Black communities in the United States, but today they seem to dismiss both their seriousness and significance for the mission and unity of the worldwide Church.

In any international study of one common expression of the Apostolic Faith there is a need for us to restate and clarify what we mean by Black theology. The Black churches must explain how the conditions of survival and liberation for people of African descent living in racist societies have, by the grace of God and the power of the Holy Spirit, given the same faith presumed to be the property of most whites a different perspective and legitimation among most Blacks. The relevant question is, what *is* this Black theological perspective and to what extent is it faithful or unfaithful to the Apostolic residuum?

III. BLACK CHURCH PRIORITIES AND THE BLACK PERSPECTIVE

What we call the Black theological perspective can also be discerned by a study of the polity and programmatic priorities of Black denominations and congregations down through the years. Our churches were rescue missions and survival stations on an underground route to freedom and dignity. The theology that thundered from the pulpits on Sundays was less concerned about how to understand the first three articles of the Nicene Creed than about faith, hope and love and their relevance to obtaining the next three meals. Our churches were also missionary outposts on the frontier of abject poverty and white hostility. As such they sent out deacons and deaconesses, teachers, Scout leaders, social workers and community organizers to encourage a dispirited people, advocate for the poor and dispossessed, and lead religious and secular movements for freedom and social justice. By examining these priorities of the churches we can arrive at an understanding of the peculiar angle from which they viewed the Gospel and the significance they gave to various aspects of faith and order.

What was important to white churches was not necessarily important to Black. White churches became embroiled in many disputes between fundamentalists and liberals, Black churches almost never. White churches emphasized peace and unity in the body and assiduously tried to avoid schisms. Black churches, despite the pain of schism, seemed somewhat better able to tolerate splits and splinter groups. Black religious institutions enjoyed luxuriant growth through a pluralism and proliferation frowned upon by white mainline churches. The white laity exercised control over most of their ministers and in the mainline churches charismatic and autocratic preachers were regarded with suspicion and disfavor. Black churches preferred strong, charismatic leaders and Black preachers brooked no interference with the freedom of the pulpit. White churches generally felt that religion and politics should not be mixed. Their frequent excuse for not taking an aggressive abolitionist position was the impropriety of encroaching upon the civil domain. Black churches usually had no such squeamishness. After some hesitation they eagerly promoted the Civil War as a holy crusade and were rarely advocates of pacifism or non-violence until the era of Dr. King. White Christians drew a sharp dividing line between the secular and the sacred. They assigned their churches to an increasingly narrow sector of daily life. Blacks, on the other hand, recognized no sharp division and their churches were cultural centers that embraced and coordinated many aspects of community life. White churches, particularly of the Protestant establishment in the Northeast, adopted the social gospel, an historical-critical approach to scripture, and sought to accomodate the faith to the Enlightenment and the Industrial Revolution. Their Black denominational counterparts, while stressing a trained ministry, were never so sanguine about theological seminaries, demythologizing the Scriptures, or making systematic and moral theology subservient to modern philosophy and ethics.

These are only a few contrasts illustrating the divergent priorities of the two churches during most of the 19th and 20th centuries. Although many of them refer to sociological differences they point to important theological causes and effects that should not be ignored. The perspective of traditional Black Christianity can be seen by focusing on these and other priorities of the Black churches which tell us what they regarded as critical for faith and order. Whether it is correct to speak of one theological perspective or of many remains, of course, an open question that Black theologians must determine by the degree of commonality and integrity they find in the beliefs and practices of Black Christians.

As an example of some issues that may be clarified by examining church priorities and may help us to formulate a Black perspective on the Apostolic Faith contained in the Creed of Nicea, here is an adaptation of a few questions from a WCC document entitled "Toward the Common Expression of the Apostolic Faith Today" (FO/81:9, August 1981).

1.   The creed confesses faith in one God. How do we explicate "one God" against our ancestral background in ATR, our historic valorization of many aspects of Islam, and the modern tendency to absolutize finite realities such as freedom, economic prosperity and national security?

2.   The creed confesses Jesus Christ, God's only begotten Son, to be "of one essence" with the Father. In view of the openness of many Black Christians to mysticism and the tran-

scendence motifs of Eastern religions, how should we explicate this claim that human salvation cannot be real without
our participation in what is divine and eternal?

3. The creed confesses that God's only Son has become human.
   How does this faith in the incarnation illumine our understanding of the Black Messiah, our incorporation into him,
   and the significance of such symbolic representations for the
   rest of the Christian family?

4. The creed confesses faith in the Holy Spirit. To what extent
   have our African and slave religions enriched our understanding of the Holy Spirit? How do we discern the Spirit
   in the Church and in the life of the world of politics, eco-
   nomics and social systems?

5. The creed confesses one holy, catholic and apostolic Church.
   How much are the Black denominations willing to sacrifice
   in order to make this Church manifest in North America?
   What sacrifices must we demand from others in order for all
   of us to experience this one Church of Christ?

6. The creed confesses one baptism for the forgiveness of sins.
   What is the significance of baptism by water and the Holy
   Spirit in Black churches? What implication does this article
   have for our acceptance of persons of other races, classes
   and creeds whom God has already forgiven in Jesus Christ?

7. The creed confesses life in the age to come. How have our
   Spirituals and gospel songs helped us lay claim to a life which
   transcends death and yet can be experienced in the here and
   now? What do the Black churches believe about heaven, hell
   and human utopias?

IV. THE NEED FOR FURTHER INQUIRY

It should be obvious by now that this brief paper barely
scratches the surface of the problems involved in answering the
question: "What is the perspective of Black American Christians
on the search for one expression of the Apostolic Faith?" Nor will
it be possible, in the discussion that took place in New York on
May 30, to do more than become acquainted with the WCC project
itself, and get some idea of what is being asked of Black churches in
the United States in preparation for the World Conference on Faith
and Order now scheduled for 1988 or 1989.

A longer discussion involving more careful preparation,
several additional papers, and a larger number of consultants is
proposed for December 14-15, 1984 in Richmond, VA. This conference will be sponsored by the Commission on Faith and Order of
the National Council of Churches, but it cannot succeed without
the full cooperation of the various Black denominations and
ecumenical agencies. A call has gone forth from Dr. David Shan-

non, president of Virginia Union and a representative of the national Baptist Convention, Inc. for wide participation in the December conference on the part of the Black denominations and Black thoelogians across the nation.

Afro-American Christians, both those within Black denominations and those within predominantly white denominations, have not been conspicuous in the World Council of Churches' studies of Faith and Order. From all indications we will be even less represented in the future because the increasing membership of the Council and the necessity of giving greater voice to Third World churches and women will probably reduce the proportional representation and visibility of Black Americans in the years to come. Black Christians do care about the visible unity of the one Church of Jesus Christ across all barriers of race and nationality. Although a few individuals have been active in the world confessional bodies and various international conferences, the churches and Black American theologians have been virtually ignored by the conciliar movement. But we must accept some responsibility for our marginality in the World Council of Churches.

This means that if an Afro-American Christian experience and perspective is to have any impact upon the world ecumenical movement it will require our theologians to take a more active role in responding to the WCC studies and initiatives. Indeed, we must take the initiative ourselves and place before the Council and the world confessional bodies the problems and issues we deem important to the mission and unity of the Church at this point in time.

At the Fifth Assembly of the World Council of Churches, meeting in Nairobi in December 1975, the following recommendation was adopted:

> We ask the churches to undertake a common effort to receive, reappropriate and confess together, as contemporary occasion requires, the Christian truth and *The timefaith*, delivered through the Apostles and handed down through the centuries. Such common action, arising from free and inclusive discussion under the commonly acknowledged authority of God's Word, must aim both to clarify and to embody the unity and the diversity which are proper to the church's life and mission. (Section II, 19)

The time is ripe for Black Christians in the United States to make our concerns and contributions known. The attempt of the churches of the world to express together a common understanding and confession of the one Apostolic Faith gives the Black Church an opportunity to share with others the wealth of wisdom and experience that God has given to it. This "gift of Blackness' comes from the long years of our struggle equally to participate in and share the ministry of Jesus Christ, a ministry which we always recognized as not only for the salvation of our own people here in the United States, but of all humanity.

BLACK CHRISTOLOGY: INTERPRETING ASPECTS OF THE APOSTOLIC FAITH

Jacqueline Grant

As I read the working paper for our discussion of confessing the apostolic faith from a Black perspective, I was struck by the christological affirmations contained within it. My response was basically affirmative of the paper but my feeling was that there was still something more to be said. Because I found myself most reflective of the christological points I felt it would be the focus of my responses.

In the following pages I shall discuss some of Black people's understanding of Jesus Christ, as reflected in aspects of the Black tradition. Because Black theologians have utilized this tradition in the development of Black Christology, I then will look at the ways in which they have interpreted the function of Jesus Christ in the experience of Black people. Finally I examined whether or not Black theologians have gone far enough in their interpretation of Christology particularly in the light of contemporary questions regarding sexism and theology. It is not my intention to be exhaustive in this examination, but merely to raise questions which I intend to explore further in another context.

1. ASPECTS OF BLACK PEOPLE'S UNDERSTANDING OF JESUS

An integral part of the classical concept of Christology was the understanding of co-eternality and co-equality of the three persons of the trinity. Augustine could say then "not only is the Father (sic) not greater than the Son in respect of divinity, but Father and Son together are not greater than the Holy Spirit and no single person of the three is less than the Trinity itself."[1] The christological importance of this is that Jesus is just as much God as God is God.

The Black Church historically has affirmed the classical christological understanding of the dual nature of Jesus Christ. Not only was Jesus fully human but he was also more than human. Jesus Christ was acknowledged to be savior and redeemer. As such he was believed to be a part of the divine reality of the Godhead.

For Black Christians, Jesus was that part of the Godhead which was accessible to them and so they spoke of him as their friend in time of need. He has been referred to as "a rock in a

---

Dr. Grant is Assistant Professor in Systematic Theology at Interdenominational Theological Center in Atlanta, Georgia.

1. J.N.D. Kelly, *Early Christian Doctrine* (New York: Harper and Row, 1960), p. 272.

weary land." In Black Gospel tradition he has been "a doctor in the sick room," "a lawyer in the court house." Jesus is one who "makes a way out of no-way." Black preaching tradition exhorts Jesus as "a shelter in the time of a storm" and "a bridge over troubled waters."

It is no accident that these descriptions of Jesus Christ are concrete ones that are related to the daily life of Black American existence. Because the oppression of Blacks manifested itself in systemic discriminatory practices which meant that they were not privy to the basic human services and protections of American democracy. The metaphors employed by Black Christians were ones which emerged out of the context in which they were forced to live. Politically disenfranchised and socially dehumanized, Blacks were and continue to be constrained by poor health care, legal services and inadequate housing. Slavery and racism created such a destitute situation for them that often the only relief was the belief that Jesus is accessible to them. Perhaps it was his humanness which made him so. Even still it was the "kind" of human that he was. From his birth to his death and resurrection, he identified with the poor, and the oppressed. Because Jesus was born in a stable and killed on a cross, Blacks were able to compare Jesus' experience with their own. And so they sang:

> Po' li'l Jesus, Hail Lawd,
> Child o'Mary, Hail Lawd,
> Bawn in a stable, Hail Lawd,
> Ain't dat a pity an' a shame.[2]

The shame was equally present at the end of his life.

> Oh, dey whupped him up de hill, up de hill, up de hill,
> Oh, dey whupped him up de hill an' he never said a mumbalin word,
> Oh, dey whupped him up de hill an' he never said a mumbalin word,
> He jes' hung down his head an' he cried.
>
> Oh, dey crowned him wid a thorny crown
> Well, dey nailed him to de cross,
> Well, dey pierced him in de side,
> Den he hung down his head, an' he died.[3]

---

2. John Lovell, Jr. *Black Song: The Forge And The Flame: The Story of How the Afro-American Spiritual Was Hammered Out* (New York: The Macmillan Company, 1972), p. 302.

3. *Ibid.*, p. 303-304.

Because the Black experience in America has been essentially a "stable" and a "cross" experience they were able to identify with Jesus and they felt that Jesus identified with them. John Lovell is correct when he says that "the slave is on familiar terms with (Jesus)."[4] According to him, Jesus represented freedom and power and therefore encouraged Blacks to strive for freedom.

"As the closest link to the Lord and God, Jesus is the slave's channel to omnipotent power, and the slave leans heavily on this power. Besides sheer power, Jesus embodies the dignity and majesty of a King and this King is the slave's friend."[5]

Black theologians have looked at the Black tradition of song, prayer, testimony, sermon and have been able to articulate christological perspectives which are peculiarly Black.

2. BLACK THEOLOGY AND CHRISTOLOGY

It is the thesis of Black theologians that Christology is constructed from the interplay of social context, Scripture and traditions.[6] Cone, in *God of the Oppressed*, crystalizes the issue in the following way:

The focus on social context means that we cannot separate our questions about Jesus from the concreteness of everyday life. We ask, "Who is Jesus Christ for us today?" because we believe that the story of his life and death is the answer to the human story of oppression and suffering.[7]

The social context for Black Christology is the Black experience of oppression and the struggle against it as well as the many celebrations of Black life.

Because historically Christology was constructed in the context of white superiority ideology and domination, Christ has functioned to legitimate these social and political realities. Essentially, Christ has been white.

The task of explicating the existence of Christ for Black people is not easy since we live in a white society that uses Christianity as an instrument of oppression. The white conservatives and liberals alike present images of a white Christ that are com-

---

4. *Ibid.*, p. 301.

5. *Ibid.*, p. 302.

6. Cone, *God of the Oppressed*, (New York: The Seabury Press, 1975), p. 108.

7. *Ibid.*, pp. 108-109.

pletely alien to the liberation of the Black community. Their Christ is a mild, easy-going white American who can afford to mouth the luxuries of "love," "mercy," "long-suffering," and other white irrelevancies, because he has a multibillion dollar military force to protect him from the encroachment of the ghetto and the "communist conspiracy.[8]

In the white church tradition, Jesus Christ has functioned as a status quo figure. This is evidenced not only in the theological imagery but also in the physical imagery of Jesus himself. In a society in which "white is right and black stays back," and white is symbolized as good and black as evil, certainly there would be socio-political ramifications of color with respect to Jesus. Gayraud Wilmore locates the origin of this color symbolism in ancient history through the development of Christianity and modern secular and religious experiences.

> It is true that it was not until justification was sought for the African slave trade that what scholars today call racism developed. But to regard racism as only the highly-reasoned, pseudo-scientific theories of the natural superiority of whites over blacks which arose in the 19th century, seems much too limiting. Some people evidently assigned a pejorative meaning to blackness long before the beginning of African slavery—for whatever reason—and if the Bible itself seems relatively free of this prejudice it is only because the Jews, after many years of residence and intermarriage in Africa, were themselves a dark-skinned people by the time the Old Testament had been written. Victims of prejudice themselves, the Medieval Jews simply consigned black people to a lower status than themselves. It was not the Jews of the Old Testament period, but Jews and Gentiles of medieval Europe—especially of Northern Europe and Great Britain—who were repelled by black skin color and African physiognomy and gave renewed vigor to the color prejudice that had been sporadic and peripheral in the ancient world.[9]

The implication that white/light is good and black/dark is evil functions not only with respect to humanity, but also with respect to human's concept of their deity. The late Bishop Joseph Johnson put the point strongly this way:

---

8. Cone, *A Black Theology of Liberation*, (New York: Lippincott., 1970), p. 198.

9. Gayraud Wilmore, "The Black Messiah: Revising the Color Symbolism of Western Christianity," *Journal of the Interdenominational Theological Center, II* (Fall, 1974), p. 9.

Jesus Christ has become for the white church establishment the "white Christ," blue eyes, sharp nose, straight hair, and in the image of the Black man's oppressor. The tragedy of this presentation of Jesus Christ by the white church establishment is that he has been too often identified with the repressive and oppressive forces of prevailing society. The teachings of the "white Christ" have been used to justify wars, discrimination, segregation, prejudice, and the exploitation of the poor and the oppressed people of the world. In the name of this "white Christ" the most vicious form of racism has been condoned and supported.[10]

To counteract this historical and theological trend, Black theologians have called not only for a new departure in theology but even more specifically for a new christological interpretation. This white Christ must be eliminated from the Black experience and the concept of a Black Christ must emerge.

The claims for the Blackness of Christ are argued by Black theologians from differing perspectives.

Albert Cleage's christological claim rests on an historical argument and leaves no room for guessing about his meaning. Postulating actual historical Blackness, Cleage argues that Jesus was a Black Jew.

For nearly 500 years the illusion that Jesus was white dominated the world only because white Europeans dominated the world. Now, with the emergence of the nationalist movements of the world's colored majority, the historic truth is finally beginning to emerge—that Jesus was the non-white leader of a non-white people struggling for national liberation against the rule of a white nation, Rome.[11]

From Cleage's perspective it is simply impossible to believe that Jesus could have been anything other than Black, given the established fact of "the intermingling of races in Africa and the Mediterranean area."[12] An alternative to Cleage's position is advanced by several Black theologians; most depend upon James Cone's interpretation which emphasizes the symbolic, not the literal importance of the Black Christ.

---

10. J. A. Johnson, "The Need for a Black Christian Theology," *Journal of the ITC, II* (Fall, 1974), p. 25.

11. Albert Cleage, *The Black Messiah* (New York: Sheed and Ward, 1968), p. 3. Patriarch Albert Cleage (Jaramogi Abebe Agyemon) is founder of the Black Christian Nationalism as practiced by the Shrine of the Black Madonna. See also *Black Christian Nationalism*. (New York: William Morrow, 1972).

12. *Ibid.*

The Black Christ is . . . an important theological symbol for an analysis of Christ's presence today because we must make decisions about where he is at work in the world. . . . To speak of him is to speak of the liberation of the oppressed. In a society that defines blackness as evil and whiteness as good, the theological significance of Jesus is found in the possibility of human liberation through blackness. Jesus is the Black Christ. . . .

The blackness of Christ clarifies the definition of him as the *Incarnate One*. In him God becomes oppressed man and thus reveals that achievement of full humanity is consistent with his being.[13]

Wilmore reinforces Cone's point by predicting the Blackness of Christ on a socio-political analysis of what it means to be Black in contemporary society and, as the symbolism of what it meant in the ancient world. Wilmore says:

To call Christ the Black Messiah is not to infer that he looked like an African, although that may well have been the case considering the likelihood of the mixture of the Jewish genetic pool with that of people from the upper Nile, Nubia and Ethiopia. Nor are we implying, by calling him the Black Messiah, that other people may not find it meaningful to speak of Christ as the White Messiah, or the Yellow Messiah, or the Red Messiah. . . .

To speak of Christ as the Black Messiah is rather to invest blackness in Western civilization, and particularly in the United States and South Africa, with religious meaning expressing the preeminent reality of black suffering and the historical experience of black people in a racist society. But more than that, it is to find in the mystery of Christ's death and resurrection a theological explanation of all suffering, oppression and an ultimate liberation. To speak of the Messiah figure in terms of the ontological significance of the color black is to provide both black people and white people, if the latter are open to the possibility, with a way of understanding the relevance of the Person and Work of Christ for existence under the condition of oppression, and to call both the Black and White Church to the vocation of involvement in the liberation of the oppressed in history.[14]

Some have retrospectively posited that Jesus' Blackness was an element of his rejection. William Eichelberger, with Cone and Wilmore, addresses the socio-political dimension and the implications of Blackness and Jesus' rejection.

---

13. Cone, *A Black Theology of Liberation*, pp. 214-215.
14. Wilmore, "The Black Messiah," pp. 13-14.

If Jesus was a Black man then it is easy to understand the kind of treatment He received; the rejection, the brutalization, and eventually death. It is very significant to go back to Jesus' trial before Pilate. The people opted for the release of a thing from jail rather than one who was a true healer and liberator. Here again I refer to color. Who are the people more offended and rejected in contemporary society? What kinds of persons and races have been rejected across the centuries?[15]

Eichelberger argues that this is reflected in the fact that through the majority race—the white race—commits more crimes in America, Blacks and people of color make up the vast majority in the prisons. He continues with this point:

It seems to me that Black people and other individuals of color have been the most frequently dispossessed, disheartened, and oppressed. When one examines the fact that two-thirds of the world is non-white, it seems to me that God who loves His creation and is concerned about His world would be more likely to choose one who is a more inclusive representative of the world populace.[16]

For Cone, Wilmore and Eichelberger the meaning of Black Christology is tied to both the historical Jesus and to the resurrected Christ. The historical Jesus is critical because it is here that we find evidence of those with whom God identifies. It was with the humiliated, the poor, and the disenfranchised that Jesus lived and worked. His teachings regarding the Kingdom were especially relevant for these oppressed peoples. For he insisted by his words and actions that "to repent is to affirm the reality of the Kingdom by refusing to live on the basis of any definition except according to the Kingdom.[17]

The resurrection of Jesus as the Christ signifies that oppression is not the end. The "resurrection is the disclosure that God is not defeated by oppression but transforms it into the possibility of freedom."[18] Specifically what this means is that "for men and women who live in an oppressive society . . . they do not have to behave as if *death* is the ultimate."[19] As Jesus conquered death so will the oppressed conquer oppression. The death and resurrection are related and significant in this way.

15. William Eichelberger, "Reflections on the Person and Personality of the Black Messiah," *The Black Church*, p. 61.
16. *Ibid.*
17. Cone, *A Black Theology of Liberation*, p. 209.
18. *Ibid.*, p. 210-211.
19. *Ibid.*, p. 211.

The historical Jesus is indispensable for a knowledge of the Risen Christ. If it can be shown that the New Testament contains no reliable historical information about Jesus of Nazareth or that the Kerygma (early Christian preaching) bears no relation to the historical Jesus, then Christian theology is an impossible enterprise.[20]

Black theologians then take the view that the historical Jesus and the Christ of faith are both integral parts of Christian reality in the Black community.

3. BLACK CHRISTOLOGY AND BLACK WOMAN

Although Black Christology focused upon the poor and the disenfranchised, Black women as women have not been consciously included as a part of this group in any specific way. Despite the fact that Black women have represented the most humiliated, and the poor of the poor, their concerns were addressed only insofar as they functioned to meet the needs of Black men and Black children. In effect, Black women qua women have been invisible.[21]

Just as in the larger Black Power/Civil Rights Movement, the primary agenda for Black theologians was the restoring of Black manhood. Black womanhood appears as an apendage of Black manhood. Jesus as the Black Messiah was a response to the emasculation of Black men with only implicit reference to the victimization of Black women. With two conspicuous exceptions, the possibility that the Christ could be Black *and* female was unimaginable. In his article cited above, Eichelberger is able to see Christ not only as Black male but also Black female.

God, in revealing Himself and His attributes from time to time in His creaturely existence, has exercised His freedom to formalize His appearance in a variety of ways. . . . God revealed Himself at a point in the past as Jesus the Christ a Black male. My reasons for affirming the Blackness of Jesus of Nazareth are much different from that of the white apologist. . . . God wanted to identify with that segment of mankind which had suffered most, and is still suffering. . . . I am constrained to believe that God in our times has updated His form of revelation to western society. It is my feeling that God is now manifesting Himself, and has been for over 450 years, in the

20. Cone, *God of the Oppressed*, p. 115.
21. Prior to Cone's article in 1976, no Black theologian had addressed the issue of women. William Jones in *Is God a White Racist?* did pose as a parallel to the charge that God could possibly be a Divine racist, that God may also be a Divine sexist (pp. 125-126).

form of the Black American Woman as mother, as wife, as nourisher, sustainer and preserver of life, the suffering Servant who is despised and rejected by men, a personality of sorrow who is acquainted with grief. The Black Woman has borne our griefs and carried our sorrows. She has been wounded because of American white society's transgressions and bruised by white iniquities. It appears that she may be the instrumentality through whom God will make us whole.[22]

Granted Eichelberger's categories for God as woman are very traditional, nonetheless he was able to conceive of God in other than a Black male messianic figure. Even before it became the expected thing to do, William Jones in challenging theodicy in the theism of Black theologians recognized the sexist aspect of Black Christology. He admonished Black theologians to avoid two extreme positions. "[H]is theodicy must be relevant to the elimination of the oppression of the groups he represents; but he must avoid reintroducing the same oppression, reverse racism for example, or a different type of oppression, such as sexism."[23] Of Cleage's use of the "image of God" as the basis of his Black God/Black Messiah notion, Jones said:

Cleage's response to white racism appears to fall prey to at least one of these dangers. His radical emphasis upon the importance of the particularity of God's incarnation will inevitably raise the issue of His incarnation in a specific human form, a male body. And here the issue of divine sexism becomes a live issue. What does Jesus' assumption of a male form imply relative to the coequal status, the cohumanity and salvation of females?[24]

Here we see Jones as early as 1973 asking, can a (black) male messiah save women?

Black christologies, in spite of the improvement made upon white male articulated Christ, still leave little hope for the liberation of Black women. The Black Christ is still primarily the male Christ. The symbol of Christ has functioned to restore the

22. Eichelberger, "Reflections," p. 54.

23. Jones, *Is God a White Racist?*, p. 126.

24. *Ibid.* Later developments in Cleage's thoughts have taken focus away from the divinity of Jesus. Jesus was divine, but not uniquely so. As Jesus made complete connection with the divine reality, so can we. There has been no recent publication which records his current thoughts which have evolved from his original views regarding Jesus. Though recent developments do not focus exclusively upon maleness, the structure of the Shrine of the Black Madonna is still basically Patriarchal. Recently, one woman bishop was appointed. (Conversations with ministers of the Shrine, Cardinal Donald Lester et al, Atlanta, Georgia.)

dignity—the divine connectedness of Black men. God has changed in color, but not in character with respect to women. The Liberator Black God has revealed *Himself* in a Liberator Black Christ who is male. Black women remain in the realm of the subordinate support structure (servant) for her man. Sojourner Truth warned us about this in 1867 when she said "There is a great stir about colored women, and if colored men get their rights, and not colored women theirs, you see the colored men will be masters over the women and it will be just as bad as it was before."[25]

What remains to emerge is some serious and consistent theological and christological construction based on the specific social context and experience of Black women which, I think, can lead to a more wholistic Christology.

---

25. Sojourner Truth, "Keeping the Things Going . . ." in Schneir, *Feminism*, pp. 129-130.

CONFESSING THE APOSTOLIC FAITH TODAY FROM THE BLACK CHURCH PERSPECTIVE

THOMAS HOYT, JR.

It is an honor to respond to the paper of one whom we all admire as a person committed to the ecumenical task. Like Professor Wilmore, we were asked to focus upon the Apostolic Faith as expressed in our various communions. The term "apostolic faith" is very ambiguous. It is similar to the phrase some append to the New Testament, namely, "apostolic writings". How is the word "apostolic" to be used? If reference is to the twelve, which of the New Testament writings come directly from one of the "twelve" apostles?

Is faith expressed in the New Testament as a whole identical with the "apostolic faith"? This would not be the case if the latter is defined in Christological terms as Martin Luther is so inclined. He says: "What does not teach Christ, is not apostolic, even if it was taught by Peter or Paul; again, what preaches Christ, this is apostolic, even when preached by Judas, Annas, Pilate and Herod."

The term "apostolic faith" is also ambiguous when it is used to cover both the faith expressed in the Bible and the faith expressed in the creeds. Some have even contended that in reaching consensus on baptism, eucharist and ministry, we have essentially arrived at agreement on the apostolic faith. We would be on safer grounds to contend that the common expression of the apostolic faith contains far more than what is confessed in worship and liturgy, but is nevertheless rooted in Christian worship and has its place there.

The statement concerning the apostolic faith by Lukas Vischer is worthy of repetition and reflection. He says:

> . . . the apostolic faith is certainly not just a fixed number of statements which can be handed down to others. It is a living message intended to be heard and proclaimed afresh, again and again. The Church must therefore be a community which is constantly wrestling with questions. At the same time, however, it must also be prepared to undertake the risky venture of giving common answers to these questions. The sacramental structures remind the Church of the source of its being and life. The ancient church creeds set before it the

Dr. Hoyt is a professor of theology at the Hartford Seminary Foundation in Hartford, Connecticut.

exemplary response of the early centuries. But if it is to be enabled to respond today with a common answer, it has to turn afresh to the living Word. The Church must seek to learn from the scriptures what it has to say today. It will seek to listen also to the answers given by previous generations through the centuries. It realizes, however, that its task remains unfulfilled so long as it does no more than repeat these answers. Only as it examines the questions raised by the contemporary situation can it really proclaim the apostolic faith.[1]

All of this emphasis on the apostolic faith and the church as a conciliar fellowship which reinterprets and confesses anew, sounds like the right words, but the Church has never come to grips with the event which caused the first conciliar meeting in Jerusalem. This meeting was called because of the Jew-Gentile problem (Acts 15 and Galatians 2:1-10). For North American Churches and beyond, the problem of Black-White relations is a major factor in the way in which the apostolic faith has been confessed and is being confessed today.

Without rehearsing the historical data which gave rise to the three predominantly Black Methodist bodies, namely A.M.E., A.M.E. Zion and C.M.E. churches (the latter representing the one to which I belong), let me make several observations. All three churches have common historical rootage and traditions in what is now the United Methodist Church. All three exist because of discrimination on the basis of race. The membership in all three is predominantly Black. All three have the same orders of ministry, and sacraments. They have a relationship in which members and ministers can transfer from one church to the other without penalty. All three have to confront problems imposed by racial conditions in the Church and community as well as problems common to all churches as institutions.

The Christian Methodist Episcopal Church has consistently confessed its faith in word and deed through its participation not only with the historic Black Methodists but through work within the World Methodist Council, the Consultation on Church Union, The World Council of Churches and The National Council of Churches.

Professor Wilmore addressed several questions as he moved toward a discussion of the apostolic faith of the Black Church. We shall list a few and speak briefly to them.

First, the question is addressed: Why do the historic Black Churches (inclusive of those in the predominantly white denominations) and their unique expressions of spirituality and worship

---

1. Lukas. Vischer, *Ecumenical Perspectives on Baptism, Eucharist and Ministry*, "Unity in Faith", p. 7.

exist? This question is answered by him in terms of isolation and marginalization from the majority; influence from the African past; life of poverty in the rural and urban centers; and struggle against racial oppression. Anyone who would at this juncture in history question whether there exists an entity called the Black Church in North America because of these enumerated reasons, is not aware of the true history of Church life in North America.

Second, the question is asked: Why does the World Council wish to hear from the Black Churches concerning their belief structure and level of commitment toward visible unity? Gayraud suggests that it is because of the Black Church's high visibility in many of the largest cities in the United States. While this is a pragmatic reason, I would hope that Faith and Order of the World Council also wishes to know what the Black Church has to offer based on their rich theological heritage which has enriched, should, and could enrich the wider Church community.

Faith and Order Commission of the World Council of Churches has already submitted to the Churches the now well-known document: *Baptism, Eucharist and Ministry*. This document represents the fruit of at least fifty-five years of ecumenical study, prayerful reflection, and dialogue among the three hundred member-churches that comprise the World Council of Churches. Responses from various churches have stressed their convergences and divergencies with the various aspects of beliefs about baptism, Eucharist and ministry. For example, the Anglicans look at baptism statements and ask, why does the BEM text read "sign" instead of "initiation", which is the word used for baptism in the Book of Common Worship. The Methodist communion and others have applauded the agreements concerning the emphasis of the Eucharist as a sign of a new eschatological reality in which Christ is the host. This fact alone means that the sacrament calls for Christians to be in mission and to live "in solidarity with the outcast and to become signs of the love of God" (par. 21). The Presbyterians and others look at the text on Ministry and observe that the document says, in the spirit of a compromise, that the tradition of those churches which do not ordain women "must not be set aside". It further suggests that those churches which do or do not permit ordination of women should learn from each other.

The point which is being stressed by highlighting a few responses to the BEM document is to suggest that each communion critiques the document based on their own statements of faith and practice. These statements of faith and practice as shaped by the Scripture have been inculcated in The Book of Common Worship, The Westminster Confession, The Articles of Faith, The Methodist Discipline, the Nicene and Apostles Creed, etc. It is remarkable that the Lima document has set forth clearly and succinctly "the major areas of theological convergence" of over a dozen church traditions, including traditions as diverse as Eastern Orthodox and Baptist, Roman Catholic and Christian Methodist Episcopal Churches, especially when each tradition feels that its faith and practice has been true to the apostolic tradition in ways that others have not. While the traditional Black Churches in North America have not entered fully into this discussion, they share in much that has been propagated by the BEM document.[2]

One gets the feeling that there is a concerted effort today to hear from the predominantly Black Churches in North America exactly because our heritage is rich and our voice has been all too silent in the world's forum. This is stated in spite of the great contribution on the world's scene by persons like James Cone, Deotis Roberts and Gayraud Wilmore, to name a few. Considering the great contribution of the latter persons to the world community, we may have to say that we have not been silent so much as ignored. Often, those with traditions which are considered by the adherents as more authentic than others refuse to recognize the God of the oppressed, and will claim that we are incapable of appreciating God's revelation.

The feeling that Blacks were intellectually and culturally inferior and their worship was thus of an inferior nature has been a part of the Methodist tradition. When evangelism was reluctantly permitted on behalf of "Negro slaves", some felt that converted slaves made good slaves. Their souls may belong to God but their bodies still belonged to the master. There were white abolitionists who considered slavery to be evil. However, the intent of some missionaries preaching among the slaves was to make the slave feel guilty about those acts considered unslavelike. Sins like lying, stealing, cheating, immorality, etc. were preached against by the white missionaries. All was intended to make the slave accept his/her condition and to await a heavenly home after this life was over. Such eschatological hope is still a part of the mentality of some Blacks today.

The converted slave in the Methodist Church was taught the Capers cathechism. William Capers' cathechism was approved as the official one among Negroes by the Methodist General Conference. The principle upon which this cathechism was based was the inferiority of the Negro slave and was intended to provide a theological justification for the slave's state of bondage and servitude. Bishop Othal Hawthorne Lakey in his book *The Rise of Colored Methodism*, gives a brief statement showing the principle upon which Capers prepared this justifying statement:

> It is obvious that much of the instruction given . . . must, of necessity, deal in the first principles of Christian truth; must to

2. See the Article by Geoffrey Wainwright, "Methodism's Ecclesial Location and Ecumenical Vocation" *One in Christ*, pp. 125-28.

a large extent, be adapted to an humble grade of intellect, and a limited range of knowledge; and must make its impression by constant and patient reiteration.[3]

John Wesley's and Capers Catechism were printed in the same volume. Some of the questions and answers were:

Q. What did God make man out of?
A. The dust of the ground.
Q. What does this teach you?
A. To be humble.

Q. What is your duty to God?
A. To love him with all my heart, and soul, and strength, to so worship him and serve him.
Q. What is a servant's duty to his master and mistress?
A. To serve them with a good will heartily and not with eye-service.[4]

It is clear that there is a feeling of superiority and paternalism being expressed toward the slave, vestiges of which are still a part of the contemporary scene. The feeling that our expression of faith had to be judged for its adequacy in the light of the standards of whites has led to some aberrations of our true selves. However, we applaud the current mood of Faith and Order which seeks to give a hearing to various traditions.

Going beyond BEM, the Faith and Order commission now wishes to take on a project entitled "Towards the Common Expression of the Apostolic Faith Today". The nature of the project implies that there is a core of Christian truth that can be identified and must be conserved. For Methodists as stated in the 1972 Discipline of the United Methodist Church: This living core . . . stands revealed in Scripture, illumined by tradition, vivified in personal experience, and confirmed by reason. As Gayraud Wilmore has suggested and as Lima has decided, the Nicene Creed has been chosen the determinative foundation for the project on the common expression of the apostolic faith today. How we respond to that creed will say a great deal about our identity as a people with a Methodist heritage.

Third, how can we as Black Churches begin to respond to the theme of Church Unity as an Expression of the Apostolic Faith? We cannot do it apart from an analysis of the effect of racism on the way Christianity is expressed among white persons and the

---

3. Quoted in the book by Othal Hawthorne Lakey, *The Rise of Colored Methodism*, (Crescendo Book Publications; Dallas, Texas) p. 37.
4. Quoted Ibid. p. 38.

manner in which Blacks have responded to that racism. Since racism is opposed to the Christian's understanding of creation and redemption, the White Church must seriously question whether it can be the Church and still carry out racist practices which deny the identity of a whole group of persons.

Among Black Churches, the core test of apostolicity is not whether one recites the creeds or is baptized but whether one is able to carry out the apostolic task. Creed and deed must go together. There is a renewed call for theologians in Faith and Order and churches in WCC to begin to take more seriously the life, ministry and teachings of Jesus Christ as the Christ who identified with the marginals of society. We have concentrated on the Pauline corpus in ecumenical circles to the extent that the synoptic traditions have seemingly been relegated to a subservient role in ecumenical documents. We seem certain of the Christ of faith motif but are skeptical of the Jesus of history emphasis. It is as if we are afraid to let Jesus live among us for that presence among the poor and outcast might judge us too harshly.

In a very pointed statement addressing this very propensity of white exegetes of the Christian faith, James Cone states:

> It is interesting that many white scholars are skeptical about the historical validity of practically everything that the Gospels record about Jesus' ministry except his political involvement. They are sure that he preached love, which they invariably interpret to mean an acceptance of the political status quo. His gospel, they contend, was spiritual or eschatological, but had nothing to do with political revolutionary struggle. This is a strange form of logic, especially since they are the same scholars who adhere rigidly to the form critical method and also universally proclaim that the kingdom about which Jesus preached included the whole of reality. Why is it that they do not express the same skepticism when dealing with Jesus' politics as they do with something else? How can they be so sure that Jesus preached the Kingdom, an all encompassing reality, but suggest that it had nothing to do with politics? How can they say that the God of Jesus was Yahweh of the Old Testament, but shy away from his political involvement on behalf of the oppressed? How could Jesus be God's representative on earth, and not be concerned about social, economic, and political injustice?[5]

After raising these rhetorical questions, Cone concludes:

> I think the answer to these questions is obvious. White theologians' exegesis is decided by their commitment to, and

5. James H. Cone, *God of the Oppressed* (The Seabury Press: New York, 1975) p. 223.

involvement in, the social structures of oppression. They cannot see the radical and political thrust of Jesus' person and work because their vision is committed to the very structures that Jesus despised. They are the contemporary representatives of the scribes and lawyers who cannot recognize the essential fallacy of their perspective.[6]

The Gospels give credence to the pattern of Jesus ministry and in turn give hope to the oppressed. We need to spend more time with the Jesus of history in order to avoid the great tendency toward gnosticism.

When one looks at the times in which Jesus lived and their social, political and economic factors, one comes to appreciate the total impact of the Gospel of Jesus Christ upon a total system. Let's take a brief look at the situation.

After the exile of the population of Israel to Babylon, Palestine was always subject to neighboring empires while being dominated from within by a rich class of landowners. Rome's domination of Palestine under Pompeii in 63 B.C. and subsequent years took several forms:

1. Economically, the people were exploited through taxes of various kinds. The official taxes drained from the Palestinian economy each year have been estimated at about 6,000,000 denarii, where one denarius is equivalent to one day of work for one worker. There were also "unofficial taxes collected by the Roman officials and their Palestinian allies.

2. There was also political domination, as the Romans sought to coordinate, facilitate, and legitimate their rule. The existing political hierarchy catered to the whims of the Roman officials. Of course, the Romans appointed at the top of the hierarchy a Roman official. In Judea it was the procurator living at Caesarea, and over Galilee it was the Roman legate of Syria who ruled through the intermediary of King Herod Antipas. The Romans ruled primarily, however, by coopting the existing political hierarchy. The procurator of Judea appointed the high priest, choosing him from one of the four powerful families. Furthermore, they enlisted the support of the large landowners and the aristocracy, if only through the threat of appropriating their property rights, and they actually recruited native Palestinians into the work of governing on their behalf; members of the high Roman administration were recruited in the aristocracy, and publicans of Jewish origin were recruited to collect the taxes.

3. The people were harrassed through military domination, the ultimate guarantor of Roman rule.

---

6. Ibid. p. 223.

4. Internally, Galilee was ruled by a high priest and the Sanhedrin. The Sanhedrin had 71 members belonging chiefly to the Sadducean Party, the families of the high priest and the elders of the aristocratic families, and the groups of scribes, Pharisees, and priests. In Galilee the Sanhedrin played the role of the Supreme Court; and in Judea it represented the supreme political power. It was the temple which served as an important seat of political power.

In addition to political power, the temple was an important seat of economic transactions. All Jews over twelve had to pay an annual temple tax equivalent to two days work; there was also a tax of ten percent of the harvest for maintenance of the Levites. The Temple also received gifts and alms, and provided the stock market for commerce in victims for the sacrifices (the revenues of which were monopolized by the four families from which the high priest was chosen.) Also associated with the Temple was the National treasury. Thus, the seat of religious and political power was at the same time an important economic power. This picture of the first century images the contemporary one. The impact of this system of economic and political domination on the majority of Jews was devastating. In the rural areas, there was no middle ground between the laborers and small land owners on the one hand, and the rich farmers, who were often absentee landlords, on the other. The dual system of taxation promoted the increasing impoverishment of the masses at the same time that the increased market for agricultural produce fattened the purses of the rich. In the cities, the workers and even the lower middle class suffered also from the double system of taxation, even as merchants and some other groups benefited from the inflation and the role of big cities like Jerusalem as centers of consumption. There were, then, three social levels in this system; the rich who benefited from taxation or at least escaped it; the hardworking poor kept on subsistence by taxation, and the destitute who had given up the unequal struggle. Sound familiar?

This exploitation had predictable effects in the lives of the people. There was widespread poverty and hunger. Many of the widespread diseases can undoubtedly be traced to this condition. Some of the blindness, for example, probably derived from poor sanitation and the unsettled lifestyle of many poor people. Like heart disease, very high among poor persons today, many of the physical illnesses and so-called cases of demon possession reported in the gospels were the natural socio-psychological responses to an alienating and oppressive situation. Inevitably, too, this situation incited a resistance movement, the Zealots, who opted for a guerilla solution against the Romans. Their aim was to restore the Jewish state, initiate a theocratic dimension, in the line of a Davidic messianism. It is clear then, that the economic, political, social, and religious dimensions of Palestinian life in this period were profoundly related and contributed to the crowds being harrassed and helpless, like sheep without a shepherd.

Contrary to popular opinion, it was Paul who protested against emphasis on the Holy Spirit or the Christ of faith which said in effect, "Jesus be anathema" meaning "Jesus be damned." This kind of emphasis on the Holy Spirit played into the hands of those who dealt with Gnosticism and a docetic Christology.

Paul comes down hard against that understanding, not by denying that Christ is transcendent, nor by denying that Corinthians have spiritual experiences. He merely asks them to take a second, critical look at those experiences. "You know that while you were still heathen you had all kinds of exotic religious experiences—yet they were false" (I Cor. 12:2). Is it the Spirit manifested in God's commitment to redeem this world and humankind in Jesus of Nazareth, and a salvation that excites not just the hope of heaven but results in the transformation of relationships here and now as well? Paul anticipated in some respects what the western Church later was to insist upon in defining the doctrine of the Trinity: "We believe in the Holy Spirit, the Lord, the giver of life, who proceeds from the Father and the Son."

The Holy Spirit revealed the Holy Spirit's form and shape in Jesus of Nazareth. The Holy Spirit is thus not to be understood apart from the life and mission, suffering and death, resurrection and exaltation of that same Jesus Christ. The experience of the Spirit must testify to the Spirit operative in the earthly Jesus. That translates into compassion for the neighbor, for the oppressed and dispossessed of the world. Gnosticism is so carried away by heavenly language and experiences that the commitment of God to this world is minimized. It ignores the incarnation or "infleshment" of the revelation. When that is done the uniqueness of Christianity is eradicated and becomes another mystery religion. The religion of Blacks in America has helped keep the Churches in North America true to the heavenly and earthly vision of Jesus Christ.

While some in the Black Church have remained skeptical of the contribution of Paul to understanding faith in the Christ, as a people we have been impressed by the way Paul deals with the tension between the Jews and Gentiles. Christ is a scandal to the Jews and foolishness to the Gentiles. He is a scandal nailed, hanged on a tree, spat upon by passersby. His death makes no sense to the Jews, being an offense against the law. Neither does it make sense to the Gentile, whose wisdom had nothing to do with the resurrection. The two views are therefore condemned on the Cross; they are incompatible and their inevitable collision led to victory of the risen Messiah, which is condemnation of both views. This confounding of both views by the offense of the cross leads to hope for those who are oppressed. Now, "there is neither Jew nor Greek, there is neither slave nor free, there is neither male nor female, for we are all one in Christ Jesus." (Gal. 3:28).

The Black Church has always known that the Bible is concerned with religious questions which are never divorced from physical ones. Human beings are to be reckoned as encompassing the totality of existence. Blacks have known this instinctively due to their quest and struggle to survive in the American society. It was out of oppression that God elected and saved Israel. So it has been with the Black Church. As such, Blacks have certain advantages as a consequence of oppression. We are taught to look critically at each other as we do at others. We are taught that not only our material, physical security is threatened, but our whole life is at stake. Those who are oppressed hear God speaking to them and are ready to listen because they have no other hope except in God. God appeared to Hagar the slave when she had no hope for the future. (Gen. 16:7-13). When the people of Israel were taken to Babylon because of their hardheartedness and rebellion against God they remembered well the message of the prophet when religion was nothing more than ritual for them (Amos 5:22-23). As it was with Hagar and Israel in Babylon, so it has been with Blacks. Yet we believe in an "Almighty Sovereign God", as Cecil Cone has so forcefully stressed.

For the African, religion is a way of life. There is not a separation of religion and a way of life. In the Western tradition one *worships* to celebrate the Almighty. In the African tradition one *lives* to celebrate the Almighty. That is not withstanding the fact that many traditional African religions are assumed to have practiced ancestor worship. The fact is that for the African, ancestors were the vessels of all earthly wisdom and knowledge.

An example of how religion was woven into everyday life is that, in certain countries, the cosmic identity (that inseparateness from God) is established at birth in the name given to the child. It is understood that at the naming, the child will become one with that moment in nature and in time. The spiritual world and objective reality come together in a manner in which the whole person is open to the divine and to all of human life.[7]

For the contemporary Black American, whose slave ancestors came out of this tradition, unquestioning faith in a supreme power is a given. In scriptural terms, through his counterpart Job, one learns that one cannot fathom the ways of God, so one must trust the trustworthiness of God even when one does not understand what God is doing in nature and in the world. Unlike Job, which

---

7. Gayraud S. Wilmore, *Black Religion and Black Radicalism*, second edition (Maryknoll, NY: Orbis Books, 1984) p. 27.

has a fairy tale and totally unsatisfactory ending in that everything seems to work out alright, for the contemporary Black American, his estate derives from faith in God.

The faith in God which sprang forth in the testimony meetings among the slaves when they met for love feasts or speakers meetings apart from their "masters" is adequately illustrated in the following slave testimony:

> My bredren, I hab my hard bone fur to chaw, an' my bitter pill fur to swaller, but bredren, I tell you what, 'ligion makes de bone turn to marrow an' de bitter to sweet. 'ligion's jus' like de spring in de back country, de furder you go de sweeter de water tastes.[8]

Finally, whether we agree or disagree, the inclination to such strong and unyielding faith in Black Americans may indeed be a racial inheritance which stems from the collective unconscious. We have this faith in God, in spite of the negative evidence of our economic, physical, and spiritual lives.

We do not hesitate to affirm, therefore, the first article of the Nicean Creed: "We believe in one God, the Father, the Almighty, maker of heaven and earth, of all that is seen and unseen." Almightiness is the power of God, uninhibited by earthly realities. It was the Almighty God who created all human beings and thus established equality of all. This has been a central cornerstone of the faith of Blacks. It was the Almighty God who elected Israel to proclaim God's love, and who sent prophets to proclaim God's love to a stubborn and wayward people. It was the Almighty God who sent God's only begotten Child to die for a sinful world and free us from oppression, sin and death. God's almightiness is beyond anything that the power of nations and persons can control. God's almightiness is the power of love. It is love that was crucified on the cross for all humanity. This power of love transcends our ethnicity and pluralism, but also unites us all, even paying the price of the cross.

Fourth, what does the Black Church share with the white Churches in terms of the apostolic witness? Among Black Methodists, we have the Articles of Religion, which have been passed down from the time of John Wesley; we believe in the Apostles and Nicene Creeds and have even placed them in our Disciplines; we adhere to the Scriptures as a source of authority for our faith; we add the Anglican and Methodist emphasis on tradition, Church, reason and experience to the scripture as our bases of authority in matters of faith. While we take all these factors into consideration, we must still agree with Gayraud Wilmore who contends that:

---

8. Quoted from W. P. Harrison, *The Gospel Among the Slaves* (Nashville, Tennessee: Publishing House of the M. E. Church, South, 1893), p. 201.

. . . although Black and White Christians received what is basically the same inheritance of the gospel, they have differed from one another in the emphasis, articulation and nuances of interpretation given both to scripture and tradition.[9]

While we have differed in matters of scriptural interpretations from the white Churches, we have been close to the white Churches in ethical conservatism. James Tinney is right to trace this ethical conservatism among Blacks to the following factors:

(1) the church's role as a socialization agent in middle-class values; (2) the church's attempt to reverse the ravaging effects of slavery on the family as a social unit; (3) the church's participation in Euro-American Christian institutions, such as denominations, seminaries, etc.; and (4) the church's concern for survival in a hostile environment where digression from white societal norms incurred neutralization.[10]

In a real sense, the Black Church has behaved in its institutional life much like the larger white Church based on some of the factors enumerated by Tinney. Yet we have stayed clear of some of the faith controversies endemic to some of the white liberal and fundamentalist churches which majored in doctrinal splits.

The Black Church has, until recently, refused to split primarily over doctrinal differences, but over power squabbles which relate to institutional matters. We have tolerated theological diversity due to several factors: The Black Church came into existence because of a basic theological protest against slavery; discrimination, segregation and racism which denied the creation of God. This theological protest eventuated into a sociological protest. Thus the Black Church did not begin with doctrinal concerns about faith and order. Rather, it was concerned about Life and Work as the same was explicated by Faith and Order.

Moreover, the Black Church was somewhat uninvolved with the white fundamentalist and liberal churches during the 1920s and '30s which meant that their doctrinal concerns did not unduly influence the Black Church. In addition, the Black Church lived its beginning in a manner similar to the early Church, via oral tradition. This factor lessened the tendency to idolize the words of scripture and thus to embroil the community into controversies dealing with inerrancy of scripture and similar concerns.

---

9. Gayraud Wilmore, "Black Christians, Church Unity and One Common Expression of Apostolic Faith" (A Working Paper revised), p. 4.

10. James S. Tinney, "Perspectives on The State of Black Religion in the U.S." (A paper presented to the 11th Annual Meeting of the Society for the Study of Black Religion, convening in Boston, MA, Oct. 21-23, 1981) p. 9.

We could belabor the point that Black and white Churches differ with each other in the way in which each have nuanced the Christian faith. In this paper we have tried to respond to the initial paper by Professor Wilmore. We have suggested that the historical struggle of Blacks in North America has created unique cultural expressions, worship patterns, economic relationships, ways of responding to the Jesus of history and Christ of faith, the Holy Spirit, and God-consciousness. In addition, we have identified with the Scripture without idolizing the book. Until recently, we have refused to split over matters of doctrine and rather have been embroiled in matters of institutional politics. Much more needs to be stated in a much more systematic fashion, but these are some initial musings on this important subject.

At this point we may be better served to look at an adaptation of a few questions from a WCC document entitled "Toward the Common Expression of the Apostolic Faith Today" (FO/81:9, August 1981). We may thereby get a handle on a Black perspective on the Apostolic Faith contained in the Creed of Nicea.

ASPECTS OF THE SPIRITUAL LEGACY OF THE CHURCH OF GOD IN CHRIST: ECUMENICAL IMPLICATIONS

LEONARD LOVETT

It was not coincidental or accidental that the Rev. Dr. Martin Luther King, Jr., civil rights activist, delivered his final speech (I Have a Dream) from the world headquarters of the Church of God In Christ Mason Temple. As one of the oldest Black Holiness-Pentecostal movements of Afro-American rootage, the Church of God In Christ (COGIC) has historically been identified with the voiceless, downtrodden and the oppressed. Black Pentecostal pioneers such as William Seymour, Charles Harrison Mason, W.E. Fuller, C.P. Jones, et. at., while not steeped in sophisticated social and political strategies or theological and ethical theory, refused to allow their personhood to become destroyed by the invectives of a racist society characterized by capriciousness and inconsistency. The personhood of Black Pentecostal leaders was sustained by a consistent spiritual prayer life which became their anchor during the dark difficult days of their pilgrimage.

During an era of rapid social change, the process of dehumanization becomes more pronounced. It was during such an era that the COGIC was founded by Charles Harrison Mason in 1897 in an abandoned cotton gin building donated by its owner in Lexington, Mississippi, sixty miles north of Jackson.

COGIC was born during a period of rapid social change when values were shifting. Historically, the downtrodden have a tendency to look to religious faith for a sense of security. While religious values change slowly and often imperceptibly, such values have found safe haven within the corpus of the Black Church where they have been conserved and sustained. Mason, the founder of COGIC, as a Baptist pastor, became fascinated with Hebrews 12:14 (Follow peace with all men, without holiness no man shall see the Lord), a passage which to this day remains the touchstone of Black Pentecostal faith and conviction.

On Denominationalism

Mason had received the experience of sanctification around 1891, and was part of a body of radical "come-outers" who formed a group referred to only as "the movement". The quest for

Dr. Lovett, pastor of the Church of the Crossroads (Church of God in Christ) in Los Angeles, serves as a member of the Adjunct Faculty at Fuller Theological Seminary teaching in the Black Ministries Program.

a "deeper understanding", and their search for "the new light" developed out of their impatience with the way things were going (or not going) within those Black mainline Protestant denominations where they held a kind of auxiliary membership. It was not uncommon to belong to a Baptist or Methodist church and maintain membership in what was then called in its infancy "the movement". Mason later came under the leadership of his close friend and companion in the Gospel, Charles P. Jones, (founder of Church of Christ Holiness, U.S.A.), who was also dissatisfied with his Church because of a similar quest. The fervent desire for personal holiness combined with a consistent attack upon denominationalism by Mason and Jones not only spawned newer religious movements, but invited persecution. C.P. Jones, writing in 1894 at Selma, Alabama, typified the prevailing mood of Black Pentecostals during this period.

> When I first gave myself to the Lord to be sanctified, I had no idea at all of taking up holiness as a fad, or an "ism", or a creed, or the slogan of a "cult". I just wanted to be personally holy. I just wished to make my own calling a election sure to my own heart by walking with God in the Spirit. As a Baptist I had doctrinal assurance; I wanted spiritual assurance, heart peace, rest of soul, the joy of salvation in the understanding of a new heart, a new mind, a new spirit, constantly renewed and confronted by the Holy Ghost. This conviction "ate me up".[1]

The quest was beyond denominational or creedal boundaries as was reflected in Jones continued attack upon the institutional churches of his day. In 1903, he wrote;

> These selfish denominational organizations are not Christ's churches. Christ's churches are indwelt by His Spirit and clothed with His power. Christ's churches are those organizations of true believers who are walking by faith in His footsteps, indwelt by His Spirit and governed by His laws. The church must be sanctified and without spot or wrinkle; and her wealth is not that of buildings and money, but of faith, and her power is not of learning and members, but of the Holy Ghost.[2]

Jones and Mason parallel Luther the Reformer in that they had no intention of leaving their respective denominations. Both were later expelled from the Baptist church for embracing their

---

1. Cobbins, O.B., *History of Church of Christ Holiness U.S.A.*, (N.Y.: Vantage Press, 1966), p. 24.
2. *Truth*, September 10, 1903, Organ No. 10, Vol. VIII, p. 4.—This publication is the product of the Church of Christ Holiness U.S.A. and only can be found in private collections by a few individuals.

seminal convictions about the Holy Spirit as enduement in the life
of believers. It was C.P. Jones who later sent Mason to investigate
the Azusa Street revival in Los Angeles in 1907. Their doctrinal differences emerged around the issue of glossolalia (tongues-speaking)
as the initial evidence of the baptism in the Holy Spirit. A schism
occurred that was never reconciled between Mason and Jones over
what was then considered a sensitive and delicate issue.

No generation can frame a scheme of doctrine which should
justly limit the belief and teaching of succeeding centuries. Each
period, each generation, each body of believers may and in some
sense must formulate a theology for itself. To suppose otherwise is
to confuse the rudimentary distinction between theology and
revelation; it is to fancy each and every council, each and every
theologian, infallible. The COGIC founding Fathers during the
infancy of the Church did not have theology or creeds on their
agenda, yet there was an intense desire to be doctrinally sound in
deed and truth. In fact, I suspect they would have been wary of
anyone raising the issue concerning the need to develop a theology
of "the movement". It was not that they were basically anti-
theological; they feared the elevation of theology to a place above
the experience of spiritual encounter. While their agenda did not
include the development of systematic theology they could live with
the traditional definition of theology as "faith seeking understanding", with the insistence that faith can never be merely formal or
intellectual (not merely a *depositum fidei* to be accepted), but that
it be profoundly experiential. Theology participates in a specific
kind of faith and not just faith in general, but the faith of a historic
community. Theology must not only imply participation in a
community, but must always speak from a specific faith.[3] The
C.O.G.I.C. as a denomination tends to embrace a belief system
which does not take into account any systematic formulations of
the faith, the consensus of Christian tradition or the massive
amount of data from theological research. In fact, the belief system
is based on a biblicism which is believed to be inspired by the Holy
Spirit, and a hermeneutic influenced by certain religious
experiences which inform the church's approach to the Scriptures
and Christian tradition. Consequently the emphasis on specific
beliefs is not the result of serious theological reflection, but rather
that which has been hammered out on the anvil of personal
experience (lived experiences). The remainder of this brief paper
will focus on specific ways in which the C.O.G.I.C., would respond
to Apostolic Faith as contained in the Creed of Nicea. The
responses are solely the author's interpretation based on an inten-
sive in-depth study of C.O.G.I.C. doctrine for his doctoral disser-

3. Macquarrie, John, *Principles of Christian Theology*, (N.Y.: Charles
Scribner and Son's, 1966).

tation that sought critically to examine the five primary Black holiness Pentecostal bodies in terms of their implications for social transformation.[4]

1.   *Faith in one God* The C.O.G.I.C. posits its belief concerning God by the way He is revealed in Nature, providence, conscience and the Word. In agreement with historic Christianity, God is perceived to be revealed in Nature and Creator and Sustainer; in providence as Regulator; in conscience as Lawgiver and Arbiter; and in Word as Redeemer, Savior, Lord and King. The Trinity is viewed as:

> The Union of Three in One, generally applied to the ineffable mystery of three persons in one God, Father, Son and Holy Ghost.[5]

They further acknowledge that the conception of the Trinity can only be apprehended through revelation; that the doctrine of the Trinity cannot be explained, but it can be believed. This body conceded that while the unity of God is made so clear in the Scriptures, and is earnestly emphasized that practical disbelief in God's unity is declared to be idolatry, yet it is equally true that the Scriptures also reveal a certain threefoldness of Nature in God which requires that He be worshiped and served as three-in-one.[6] This notion does conform to the belief in the essential unity and allows for a distinction of plurality in the godhead. The Scriptures ascribe divine titles, attributes, and worship severally to the Father, the Son and the Holy Spirit.[7] Paternity is never ascribed to the Son, and filiation never to the Father, and neither to the Spirit. Finally the belief concerning God is summarized as follows:

> Thus we learn that God is one while He is three and three while He is one. He is one in Nature, essence and being, while in this one Nature, or being, He has a three-fold personality of persons. There can be no doubt that the Scriptures reveal this to us as the Mode of God's being or existence.[8]

C.O.G.I.C. views this feeling about God to be consistent with what the Scriptures reveal about God's nature. God is viewed as a dynamic personal Being who not only knows, but can be known.

---

4. Lovett, Leonard "Black Holiness-Pentecostalism: Implications for Ethics and Social Transformation", (Unpublished dissertation, Emory University, 1979).

5. *Official Manual Church of God In Christ*, (No place, 1957), O. T. Jones, Sr. and J. E. Bryant (Compilation and editorial commission), p. 46.

6. *Loc. Cit.*

7. *Ibid.*

8. *Ibid.*

God is never perceived as some static impersonal force in the universe. God is perceived to be so concerned about the total well-being of the oppressed that He will fight on their behalf "taking off chariot wheels" if need be in order to thwart the plans of the oppressor. The founder, Mason, was jailed but never convicted for preaching Hebrews 12:14, and charged with being anti-patriotic during war time. But, "God was with him" is the final commentary during his pilgrimage.

Jesus Christ the Son of God

The C.O.G.I.C. historic belief can be viewed in light of a controversy that wracked the classical Pentecostal movement during its infancy. The controversy, sometimes referred to as the "Jesus only" issue, "The New Issue", the "Pentecostal Unitarian question" and the "Oneness Issue", simply asserted that there is but one holy eternal Spirit of God. G. T. Haywood, an early exponent of this view, believed that traditional theology had got this truth badly confused. He further contended, after searching the Scriptures, that the Apostles were not divided on the issue, but that "all recognized that the Spirit of the Father, the Spirit of the Holy Ghost, and the Spirit of His Son were different expressions of the one and selfsame Spirit.[9] In response to Elder L. A. Bell of Starkville, Mississippi, who stated that "Jesus was the name of the godhead, C. H. Mason, founder of C.O.G.I.C. remarked that Jesus was the Name of the Son of the godhead and Jesus is the Son of the godhead and the Holy Ghost is the glory of His all being in the godhead."[10]

C.O.G.I.C. identifies with the notion that God clothed Himself in mortal flesh in the person of Jesus Christ: That the Holy Spirit incarnated Himslf in the humanity of Jesus. In the words of Howard Ervin, "rather than the human conforming to the divine, the interaction of the two in Christ Jesus transformed the human, making the infinite attributes of God intelligible to finite minds. C.O.G.I.C. adherents view Jesus as the one who baptizes us in the Holy Spirit. Jesus is viewed as the Son of God, the second person of the triune godhead.[11]

The Holy Spirit

It is the way in which belief in the Holy Spirit has been appropriated that has distinguished the Church of God in Christ.

9. Dugas, Paul, *The Life and Writings Elder E. T. Haywood*, (Stockton, CA: Apostolic Press, 1966).

10. *Yearbook of the Church of God In Christ*, (N.P., 1926, compiled by Lillian B. Coffey, copy in Lovett private collection).

11. *Church of God In Christ Manual*, (Memphis, Tenn.: C.O.G.I.C. Publishing House, 1973), p. 47 (Revised edition).

Indeed the baptism in the Holy Spirit is perceived to be the crowning experience for all believers and without it, one's witness is ineffective. It is the mountain top experience, for in it (the baptism in the Holy Spirit) God comes to dwell with His creation immanently in power, unction and glory. C.O.G.I.C. adherents have had very little if any concern about the famous controversy on filioque of the trinitarian disputes of the fourth century which led to the affirmation of the Spirit's divinity as the third person of the Trinity, but rather how the Spirit could energize their being with *dunamis* and *exousia* for witness in the world. They were not at all involved in the debate of the fourth century when the Greek Cappodocian Fathers laid the groundwork for later discussion of equal hypostases (persons) and the identity of the divine *ousia* (substance), but whether Christ's Churches are indwelt by His Spirit and clothed with His power. Their preoccupation was not the wealth of the church, of its buildings and money, "but that its wealth be of faith and her power derived not from learning and members but of the Holy Spirit." Herskovits argued that "spirit possession" in some African cultures was descriptive of the same religious experience transposed in western culture as the baptism of the Holy Ghost. C.O.G.I.C. sees this experience as one which empowers us to change the world. This fact has tremendous implications for social change.

Water baptism in the C.O.G.I.C. is given only to new believers as a symbol to denote cleansing of sin as the result of regeneration which already has occurred. The C.O.G.I.C. believes that in regeneration, the Holy Spirit is experienced in his introductory ministry, but in the baptism in the Holy Spirit, the believer experiences the Spirit's empowering ministry. That is why the baptism in the Holy Spirit is viewed as the spiritual baptism where Jesus, the baptizer, exercises His sovereign will, control and possession of us through the person of the Holy Spirit. C. H. Mason believed according to Scripture (Hebrews 9:22) that "without the shedding of blood, there is no remission of sin." Mason asked, "Beloved, understandeth thou what thou readeth?" Not, without the dipping into water there is no remission, but the "shed" blood. Nor does it say the water washes away our sins.[12]

Church Universal

Dietrich Bonhoeffer, German theologian and martyr, once referred to Black holiness-Pentecostals as the "stepchildren of church history,"[13] a designation which indeed merited attention,

---

12. *Yearbook of the Church of God, Loc. Cit.*, p. 26.
13. Bonhoeffer, Dietrich, *"Bericht uber den Studienavfenthalt"* in Union Theological Seminary in New York, in *Gesammelte Werke*, Munich, Kaiser-Verlay, 1958), p. 97.

because of neglect. Historians would do well to recall that C. H. Mason, founder of C.O.G.I.C., received his baptism in the Holy Spirit in a revival that eventually became so ecumenical in its thrust that an eye-witness indicated that after the Spirit came, the color line was washed away in the blood.[14] The C.O.G.I.C. affirms unequivocally that "the color line was overcome by the blood." It is in praxis that the pentecostal effusion and encounter invades the human spirit, purging away the vestiges of pride which constitute the basis of the problem of the color line. The perennial problem of the "color line" within the church in 1984 in subtle ways continues to be a spiritual problem which reflects the depths of the crises we are a part of, and requires a theological and spiritual solution. Mason was an "Azusa Street Revival" graduate, a meeting that constituted a watershed in the history of revivalism. William J. Seymour responded to the challenge of a bolted door, thereby transforming it under the guidance of the Holy Spirit into an international gateway. Without instruments, choir, collections, advertising campaigns, public relations techniques or organized church support, persons from thirty-five nations heard and responded to the message and work of the Holy Spirit, many returning to evangelize their native land. No revival prior to its time bore such interracial, international and ecumenical fruits. In time the Azusa Street Revival initiated by Black leadership at the grass roots level became not only a contribution from the ghetto to the world but also symbolic of a microcosm of pentecostal and ethnic ecumenicity. With the coming of the Holy Spirit, denominationalism and racial barriers were overcome, thus providing a model for the future. The charismatic renewal movement worldwide is indebted to a small group of Black wash women who dared to pray as they hungered for the Holy Spirit. To this day the C.O.G.I.C. has maintained an open fellowship from its inception. The C.O.G.I.C. is at home with the notion of one holy, Apostolic church where Jesus the baptizer is Lord, to the glory of God. The values born of that early redemptive community of faith among Black Pentecostals might very well become the paradigm for developing a strong sense of community in the larger Black community.

Eschatology

Within the perspective of religious history, the C.O.G.I.C. is in many ways akin to the spiritual heritage of the Radical Reformation in its attempt to combine zeal with the primitive Christian impulse towards a life of holiness which had roots in the

---

14. Bartleman, Frank, *What Really Happened At Azusa Street?*, Editor, John Walker, (Northridge, CA: Voice Publications, 1962).

New Testament Pentecostal event. C.O.G.I.C. adherents are ideologically pessimistic toward the present world order and continue to believe in a literal second coming of the Lord to this earth. We believe that the Bible alone supplies us with the only authentic revelation of the future of saint and sinner alike.[15]

C. H. Mason saw storms as a kind of interim judgment of God. Mason often preached or commented from Nahum 1:2-3, that the "Lord would have His way in storms," and the judgment of God was directed against the proud and haughty. While the denomination he founded believed in the literal return of Christ, "when the Church, the Bride, shall be caught up to meet the Lord in the air," Mason tended to focus more on God's interim judgment against the pride of man. This was revealed in several sermons.

> God, with the hand of the storm shall cast to the earth proud folks . . . National pride bringing forth wars and polluting the land, causing blood to touch blood; all of the character God will work with in storms, earthquakes and great noise, and with flames of devouring fire.[16]

Concluding Postscript

There is a need in the C.O.G.I.C. to develop a more broadly-based charismatic understanding of the Christian life that will focus on the utilization of the gifts and graces of the Holy spirit beyond itself. If discipleship involves risk for the sake of the kingdom, it must occur if it means denying oneself and embracing His will, purpose and mission in the world. Our world stands in need of humanization. When life-giving and life-sustaining values suffer increasing resistance and erosion in a society dominated by high technology, indeed there is a need for a unique kind of witness that will result in a more humane lifestyle. The C.O.G.I.C. must borrow from its past as it seeks to transform the present. The power and presence of the Holy Spirit dispensed to C.O.G.I.C. fathers a deep sense of infinite worth, a feeling of irrevocable human dignity which gave them the power and authority to keep on "keeping on" even while living on the bare edge of human existence. They did not attempt to possess the Holy, they allowed the Holy to possess them. Any attempt to possess the Holy leads inevitably to egocentrism, but to be possessed by the Holy, the "numinous" is to encounter an experience where one's awareness and sensitivity is increased. "Woe is me" must always precede "Here am I" before one's consciousness can indeed be liberated for service in the world. It was such dignity which empowered the

15. *Church of God In Christ Manual*, 1973, p. 68.
16. *Yearbook of Church of God in Christ*, 1926, p. 9.

C.O.G.I.C. fathers with a humanizing witness at the turn of the century during one of the most racist periods in our history.

A humanizing witness is one which is demonstrated rather than logically analyzed or defined. For the real issue is not whether God can use base things to confound the wise and the mighty, but whether He in fact *is* and *does* in our time. C.O.G.I.C. adherents were known for their grass roots communal concerns, though in non-institutional ways. Long before professional social workers were in vogue, praying church mothers and missionaries were taking care of the needs of the indigent, sick and poor on a purely voluntary basis, grounded in their basic religious and spiritual commitment. From "brush arbors" to storefronts, and from storefronts to cathedrals, C.O.G.I.C. adherents have come. As "stepchildren" of American religious history, C.O.G.I.C. believers know the pain of being relegated to positions of disfavor for being Black, poor and pentecostal, a condition of triple-jeopardy. Having lived between the tensions of such jeopardy and the demands of one's faith stance has sharpened the witness of C.O.G.I.C. adherents. Being a humanizing witness is far more inclusive than "testifying" in a group setting about the goodness of the Lord. It also means demonstrating the good for persons against injustice; it means to become purveyors of a love which neutralizes brute force which exploits and dehumanizes persons. No jail can incarcerate a humanizing witness which insists on sharing and demonstrating a love on fire which bears the efficacy of the grace of God in humanizing this world.

Finally, C.O.G.I.C. adherents are heirs of a legacy of spirituality which is grounded in realism. C.O.G.I.C. adherents learned from experience the value of affirming an experience in order to authenticate one's being in the world. They too share an affinity with African religion in terms of its wholistic religious worldview. For within the vortex of the Black religious experience, religion is life and is to be lived, and life is religious in the sense that we indeed look beyond ourselves for sustenance and survival. C.O.G.I.C. adherents made such a transition in their pilgrimage by their total reliance on the "Spirit" to work things out. Life to be sure was not to be compartmentalized. To "dance in the Spirit" is to participate in a celebrated victory that has already been won in history in preparation for a future "yet to be", and at the same time, recognize the power of God as the demonic is confronted in the *eternal now*. For when C.O.G.I.C. believers sing, it is the continuation of the victorious affirmation of what is taking place in life. To sing "He brought me up out the miry clay, He placed my feet on a rock to stay" is profoundly to acknowledge in grace a presence who will do whatever is necessary to help you remain "a soldier in the army of the Lord." Such is the legacy of the C.O.G.I.C. to our time. If appropriated by the grace of God, it can help make a difference in our time.

THE HOLY SPIRIT
AND LIBERATION:
A BLACK PERSPECTIVE

J. Deotis Roberts

> "And in the Holy Spirit, the Lord and life-giver, who
> proceeds from the Father, who is worshipped and glorified
> together with the Father and Son, who spoke through the
> prophets; and in one, holy, catholic, and apostolic Church."
> (Nicean/Constantinopolitan Creed)

A theological discussion which takes contextualization seriously must consider the unique contribution of Black church
Theology. I have selected a much neglected doctrine—the doctrine
of the Holy Spirit—for its Pan-African significance and its importance in itself.

Our focus is on the relationship between the doctrine of the
Holy Spirit and human liberation. What is the connection between
charismata and personal and social transformation? The African-
Afro-American holistic religious understanding does not endorse
the Western-oriented division between the personal and the social
or the physical and the spiritual. There is an assumed interpenetra-
tion in both instances. Thus we must consider here how the nature,
presence and power of the Holy Spirit are to be understood in a
meaningful way in the Black church tradition.

I. *Why the Black Theologian Must Discuss the Holy Spirit*

There is much "spirit-talk" today. Many questions are being
asked about this cardinal doctrine of the Christian faith. Recently,
I received a letter raising the questions: "Why are not liberation
theologians writing about the Holy Spirit? Is there no spirit talk
among the liberation theologians, Black feminists or Latin
Americans?" Given this challenge, I began looking for the answer
to these questions in the literature, including my own writings. My
candid answer had to be that little direct attention has been given to
this subject in the liberation theology literature.

A Black colleague of mine who has given much attention to the
doctrine of the Holy Spirit, was approached by me for his opinion.
He readily agreed that the Holy Spirit had been neglected in recent
Black theology. He noted that my first book on Black theology,
Liberation and Reconciliation,[1] had given some attention to the
subject, but that it was inadequate. But there is no gainsaying the

---

Dr. Roberts teaches theology at Eastern Baptist Theological Seminary in
Philadelphia, Pennsylvania.
1. *Liberation and Reconciliation* (Philadelphia: Westminister, 1971), p. 127.

importance of the Holy Spirit in the Black Church tradition. If the worship among most Blacks is satiated with the presence of the Spirit, the worship of the more cultured and educated Blacks often suffers from the Spirit's absence. In both cases there may be a need for deeper understanding. My warning is that the spirits be tested to discern whether they be of God. The more recent situation presents a more complicated outlook.

We focus our discussion by the use of an example. Eldridge Cleaver, who wrote in the late '60s a work entitled, *Soul On Ice*, wrote a later book called *Soul On Fire*. In the earlier period, Cleaver expressed forcefully the disenchantment which many Black militants and/or intellectuals felt regarding the quietism of Black religion. The Black churches were seen as comfort stations and havens of escapism. Cleaver was quoted often by Black militants who saw Black religion and the churches as the last bastion of Uncle Tomism. Today, however, Cleaver represented the so-called "born again" company of Blacks and whites who claim to have received a Second Blessing, the outpouring of the Spirit in their souls. One has to raise some doubts as one observes that this former Black militant gained his freedom because "a born again gambler" offered a $100,000 bail on his behalf.[2]

The example of Cleaver, of Black militants deprogrammed by religious fervor, is more widespread than we might want to admit. But what is more disturbing is the influx of young intellectuals into highly emotional religious movements in the name of the Holy Spirit. This includes not merely bright students, but Black faculty members and professionals as well. This is usually associated with an other-worldly outlook which does not fit the holistic orientation of the Black church tradition.

There are those who would question my judgment that this is an unhealthy trend, but I would argue that usually when Blacks turn away from a concern for socio-eco-politico aspects of liberation in their religious life, someone has been tampering with them. I believe there are good reasons for initiating the discussion on the Black church from this angle of vision. We need to open up the discussion of the presence and power of the Spirit in the Black church from these perspectives. You are to be reminded that earlier we suggested that the spirits must be "tested." Furthermore, the true spirit of God bears clearly discernable "fruits" in the life of the believer. Before returning to the Black church "in the power of the Spirit," we need now to look at the doctrine of the Holy Spirit.

II. *What is the Holy Spirit?*

We begin with the etymology of the word "Spirit." The Hebrew *ruach*, the Greek *pneuma* and the Latin *animus* point to

---

2. Cf. *Soul on Fire* (Waco, Texas: Word Books, 1978), p. 227 with *Soul on Ice* (New York: Dell, 1968).

the movement of air. These words are often translated as "wind," "storm," "breeze." The movement of the air is usually caused by "breath" and hence in the metaphorical the meaning shifts from "breath" to the "principle of life" or "vitality." Humans and animals have *ruach*, but God preeminently has *ruach*. He is a breathing, living and acting God. In creation God bestows *ruach* upon his creatures. Humans receive God's *ruach* to the highest degree—human life results from the breathing of God. Wherever God acts, *ruach* is at work. God's action as the presence and power of *ruach* is prevalent in the Old Testament.

The Greek New Testament continues the same basic meaning of Spirit. *Pneuma* is the sign of human vitality. Greek has two words for the human spirit: *nous* which refers to "mind" or "intellect" and *pneuma* which points to the dynamic principle of life. The New Testament leans toward the Old Testament background in spite of the metaphorical and philosophical meanings employed. John writes: "The spirit blows (*penuma pnei*) where it wills . . . so it is with every one who is born of the Spirit (*pneuma*)." (John 3:8).

In sum, we may assert the following: Spirit means that God is a vital, acting God. He grants life and vitality to his creation. The human *ruach/pneuma* is God's inspiring breath by which he grants life in creation and re-creation. God is in action in human life. The *pneuma* of a human being is his/her *dynamis*—person in action. The *pneuma* of God is God acting in Creation, providence and redemption.[3]

III. *Pneumatology and Christology*

We need to see the spirit in relation to our understanding of Jesus Christ. Berhoff's discussion is useful on this point. He sees a double relation between the Spirit and Christ. In the first instance the Spirit is said to have a priority over against Jesus. Jesus is described as the bearer of the Spirit. The Synoptic Gospels point up this relation between Jesus and the Spirit. In accordance with the prophecies it was expected that the Spirit would rest upon the Messiah. The Messiah was referred to as the Anointed One because God had anointed him with his Spirit. This association of the presence and power of the Spirit with Jesus is illustrated by passages in Matthew, Luke and Acts.[4] This view is widespread throught the New Testament.

Paul and John emphasize another relation between the Spirit and Christ because the life-giving Spirit is given attention by these authors. Paul writes concerning the Spirit as the Spirit of Christ or

---

3. See Hendrikus Berkhof, *The Doctrine of the Holy Spirit* (Atlanta, GA: John Knox Press, 1976), pp. 13-14.

4. See, e.g., Matthew 1:20, 4:1; Luke 4:14, 10:21 and Acts 1:2, 10:38, Cf. John 3:34 and Romans 1:4.

the Spirit of the Son (Romans 8:9, II Corinthians 3:17; Galatians 4:6; Philippians 1:19). John writes that Christ refers to the Spirit "whom the Father will send in my name (the Counselor) to you" (John 16:7), "whom I shall send to you from the Father" (15:26). In John (20:22) the risen Christ, by breathing on the Apostles, transmits to them the Holy Spirit. Again the relation of sender which is predominant in John and Paul is not absent from the Synoptic Gospels and Acts. See, for example, Luke 24:49, Acts 2:33. These two relations of Christ and the Spirit are complementary. Jesus is the sender of the Spirit because he has first been the receiver and bearer of the Spirit.[5]

Theologians have not held these two aspects of the doctrine of the Holy Spirit together. Those who seek to lift up the humanity of Jesus have stressed Jesus as bearer of the Spirit. On the other hand, those who exalt the divinity of Christ have stressed him as one who sends the Spirit as a gift to the church. This trend is clear from the adoptionists at the end of the second century until the Liberals of today.

It is important to develop a Christology from an understanding of the Spirit of God which combines these two relations of Jesus as "bearer" and "sender" of the Spirit of God. From a reading of the Old Testament, we understand that Jesus Christ is to be what H. Wheeler Robinson refers to as "a corporate personality." The whole of Israel and even of humankind is summed up in Jesus as the Servant of the Lord, the Messiah, the Son of Man, the Last Adam. Jesus is conceived by the Spirit, guided by the spirit, filled with the Spirit. The Spirit rests on Jesus and goes out from Jesus. The one on whom the Spirit remains, baptizes with the holy spirit.

The early attempts at developing a Christology used this pneumatic approach. This tendency may be noted in the Apostolic Fathers, e.g., Ignatius, Second Clement and the Fifth Parable of the Shepherd of Hermes. Hermes asserts that God made the Holy Spirit, which existed before creation and which participated in the entire creation, dwelling in a flesh which he ordained. This enfleshment of the Spirit, according to Hermes, "served the Spirit well in a behavior of purity and virtue, without casting any stain on the Spirit."[6] Hermes assumes that the flesh, the human nature of Christ, after his earthly work, was exalted and elected to the fellowship of the Spirit.

Around the middle of the second century there is a dying away of this development of Christology from pneumatology. Titianus in his "Speech Against the Greeks" (circa A.D. 65) used *Ruach* and *dabar* as almost synonymous. Even so his discussion is a key turn-

---

5. Berkhof, *Op. Cit.* pp. 17-18.
6. Pastor Hermae, *Similitudo*, V. 6, 5.

ing point in which Christian apologists began to prefer *Logos*
rather than *Pneuma* as their foundational concept. *Logos* was a
popular philosophical concept at the time. The use of this later concept made the Gospel more acceptable for the intellectual contem-
poraries of these theologians. Thus pneumatic Christology was
replaced by logos Christology. But his reliance upon Hellenistic
cosmology distorted the biblical basis for Christology and led to its
impoverishment. Logos-Christology prevailed and is the essence of
the church's christological formulations. It is important, therefore,
to ask whether we should not re-assess pneumatic Christology and
its support in the biblical record.[7] I would insist, emphatically, that
we should relate pneumatology to Christology and hold a
christological view of Pneumatology. Only thus may we come out
with a sound doctrine of the Holy Spirit.

IV. *The Holy Spirit and the Second Blessing*

We need to raise the issue concerning whether Pentecostalism
today is consistent with the outpouring of the Spirit at Pentecost.
Another way of raising the issue is to ask whether the baptism in
the Holy Spirit is distinct from conversion. Is it a second blessing?
Are those who believed themselves to be true Christians, but who
have no evidence of "a second blessing", deceived? Even if they
live a Christian lifestyle, must they feel inferior, without the
tongues-speaking gift? Have those who have the "second blessing"
the right to judge the deficiency in others or feel superior in com-
parison to those who have not been thus favored by God? This
detailed inquiry is the more important since Blacks are often emotional in their religious cult expression and are attracted greatly
towards the Pentecostal movement.

The Pentecostal movement believes that it has found in the
Acts of the Apostles, in its evangelical forbears and in its own
personal and missionary experience, precedent and authority for its
basic belief. Pentecostals assert that the baptism in the Holy Spirit
is a critical experience subsequent to and/or distinct from conversion, granting the believer the benefits of a permanent, personal,
and full indwelling of the Holy Spirit and so providing power for
Christian service, particularly evangelistic service, with the equip-
ment of spiritual gifts.

Bruner describes the experience of the second blessing at the
center of Pentecostalism as follows:

"A Christian is believed to be given personal graces . . . as a
result of his initial faith, but the ministering gifts, the charismata
(e.g., I Corinthians 12:8-10) are not fully given until the latter
bestowal."[8]

---

7. Berkhof, *Op. Cit.* pp. 19-21.
8. Frederick Dale Bruner, *A Theology of the Holy Spirit* (Grand Rapids, MI: Eerdmans, 1970), p. 75.

The Pentecostal conditions are necessary both to explain and to obtain the subsequent baptism in the Holy Spirit with its glossolalic evidence. The source of the doctrine of conditions is in Acts and other biblical passages which teach a connection between the gifts of the Spirit and conversion, obedience, prayer and faith. Again Bruner provides a helpful account:

"Conversion is the dispensable pre-condition for the Pentecostal baptism. Obedience—both active (with the goal of the sinless heart) and passive (with the goal of self-emptying)—is the Christian's essential preparation for the baptism in the Holy Spirit. When the obedience is complete the Christian should have faith. The faith which Pentecostalism prizes in this connection is not usually identical with initial Christian faith; it is a different kind or at least a different act of faith, directed primarily toward the Holy Spirit with a quantitative intensity, and is as such neither *sola* nor *simplex*. It is a faith added to a preparatory commitment necessary for acquiring and for appreciating the gift of the Holy Spirit. Pentecostal faith is best described as *ultima fides*."[9]

The critique of Bruner is also very helpful and worth mentioning here. The Pentecostal evidence replaces the demand for circumcision in the early church, according to Bruner. Paul confronted forthrightly this party at Corinth with a rejoinder. We note that the Judaistic evidence of circumcision and the Pentecostal evidence are supplements to initial faith and are required to receive God's favor and/or power in a complete sense. Likewise they are momentary physical phenomena, occurring at specific bodily organs, and both seem to have guaranteed, as it were, *ex opere operato*, the reality which each purports to verify. That is to say, in both cases the physical event is invested with spiritual importance.[10]

There is a distinct danger. The supplement to faith easily becomes faith's center. This was true of the "circumcision party" in Paul's days (Galatians 2:12) as well as of the "tongues movement" today. The supplement to faith becomes an advancement beyond faith and lays claim to a higher type of Christian experience. Bruner's concern is, therefore, that any supplement to faith cancels "the sole necessity of faith." Christ is no longer sufficient in his atoning work. Faith sealed in baptism is no longer adequate. It renders the saving power of the cross and the Gospel empty. It is salvation by works rather than by faith alone.[11]

My response to all this is that Bruner's critique is well taken up to a point. But as for me, the distinction he makes between faith and works, God's grace and human responsibility, is disturbing. To use a metaphor, the cure is worse than the sickness. Aren't there

9. *Ibid.*, pp. 114-115.
10. *Ibid.*, p. 282.
11. *Ibid.*, p. 283.

both human and divine dimensions to redemption? Faith and works are interdependent. The concerns of Bruner regarding Pentecostalism are echoed by Paul D. Opsahl, from the Lutheran point of view. Again faith and works and law and Gospel are juxtaposed.[12] In both cases inadequate attention, if any, is given to ethics and social responsibility. In the case of Pentecostalism we are dealing with a supplement to saving faith which is questionable. But in the critique of Bruner and Opsahl we are introduced to a concept of faith which is incomplete—it leaves out ethics, especially a "public ethic."

In Pentecostalism the Indwelling Spirit or the Second Blessing is the result of sinlessness, prayer, obedience and the laying on of hands. Passively, sinlessness is required. Actively, a life of absolute obedience is demanded. Holiness is viewed not as growth toward spiritual maturity but as sinlessness. Obedience is absolute and takes little notice of human free-will as essential to selfhood. Those receiving the Second Blessing have a privileged stance—a kind of inside track on God's grace. Other Christians and churches are in a second best position. Pentecostalism is for the "twice-born," not for those who experience the life of faith as a still, small voice or a gradual experience of sanctification, however saintly the life.

In spite of all its emphasis upon personal moral perfection, its virtues are often negative and private. It is notoriously short on social conscience and social justice. Corporate sins are seldom conceived and there is little concern for social transformation. Thus my objection to the claims of Pentecostalism is based upon ethical rather than purely evangelical grounds. I do not have a problem with a faith that lends to works as long as it has a Gospel foundation. That is to say, as long as God and humans are co-laborors together for good. I do not view a non-theistic humanism as adequate. But I do seriously question the claim to a superior knowledge of God by any individual or group. Furthermore, this claim is too often accompanied by more heat than light—a zeal not always according to knowledge or a less exemplary moral life. My concern is for a different type of evidence for the saintly life. It is the relation between *root* and *fruit* both in the private life and in the public domain.[13]

V. *Pentecostalism: A Critique from Black Theology*

Black Pentecostals are frequently concerned about "the social

---

12. Paul D. Opsahl, ed. *The Holy Spirit in the Life of the Church* (Minneapolis: Augsburg, 1978).

13. Cf. Erling Jorstad, ed. *The Holy Spirit in Today's Church* (Nashville: Abingdon, 1973). See especially pp. 71-76 where the "Second Blessing" is discussed. This work is comprehensive. It provides varied opinions by Pentecostals and non-Pentecostals as well as valuable case studies.

implications of Pentecostal power.''[14] And they are concerned
about the "exclusivist tendencies in Pentecostal self-definition.''[15]
Goodwin puts his concern this way:

"The question facing Pentecostals is: How can the power that
is continually experienced within the church fellowship be brought
to bear on problems God's children are continually experiencing
outside the church?''[16]

Tinney argues that certain tongue-speaking denominations
which have had more access to wealth and mass media have
launched an effective, exclusivistic campaign to define
"Pentecostal" in a very narrow theological, racial and cultural
sense. In a word, he is concerned about the racism which has
infested the Pentecostal Movement.

We will deal first with Tinney's concern. This I believe is
related to the convenient privileged focus of Pentecostalism. If
racism had not infiltrated the ranks of Pentecostalism, its social
consciousness might have developed along more positive lines.

First, racism in Pentecostalism is *historical*. When the Azusa
Street revival was only a month old, white Pentecostals levied
accusations against Seymour and his Black followers. Whites
claimed, rather, Parham's Topeka glossolalic event as the genesis
of Pentecostalism in this country. The history of the movement is
aimed at making white Pentecostals the only legitimate bearers of
the title.[17] Black writers view the matter differently. Lovett writes:

"The twentieth-century Pentecostal Movement in America
originated from the womb of the black religious experience. From a
converted livery stable in the ghetto on Azusa Street in Los Angeles
in 1906 to the world, the Pentecostal Movement has ushered in the
era of the Holy Spirit. Once again God has used a 'saving moment'
from the ranks of the despised and oppressed people of the earth to
inject new life and power into the church universal.''[18]

It is not so much the genesis of the movement which bothers
the Black writers. It is rather the rejection of the authenticity of the
Black movement by the whites and their blatant attempt to
overlook it. The assumption is that only the white movement is
legitimate and Blacks are a part of it, that concerns the Black
Pentecostals. A case in point is that white writers stress that

14. See Bennie Goodwin, "Social Implications of Pentecostal Power" *Spirit*
(Vol. 1, No. 1, 1977), pp. 31-35.
15. James S. Tinney, "Exclusivist Tendencies in Pentecostal Self-definition: A
Critique from Black Theology," *Journal of Religious Thought* (Vol. 36, No. 1,
1979) pp. 32-33.
16. *Ibid.*
17. Leonard Lovett, "Perspective on the Black Origins of the contemporary
Pentecostal Movement," *The Journal of I.T.C.* (Vol. I, No. 1, 1973) pp. 39-40.
18. *Ibid.* p. 42.

Seymour was a disciple of Parham, but they desire to ignore the fact that many white ministers were ordained by Bishop Charles H. Mason, founder of the Church of God in Christ. White writers also like to speak of interracial fellowship. But how can one refer to sincerity of true fellowship when whites refused to defy laws, mores and prejudices and serve under Black leaders?[19]

Secondly, racism has influenced the theology of Pentecostalism. The accepted theological position is that scriptural revelation is final and without error amongst most white Pentecostals. Not only is reason doubted, but even the Spirit is not trusted to lead to any new truth. Yet is is just at this point that Black and African tongue-speaking bodies depart from "orthodoxy." Claims to new revelations are frequent and often figure into the formation of new organizations. Black Pentecostals have been formulating a black theology for a long time. They have relied on oral traditions, African cultural retentions and the like. Blacks join African, Latin American and Asian tongue groups in rejecting the definition of whites. Whereas whites limit themselves to a fundamentalist-evangelical theology, others find it inappropriate to subscribe to this exclusivistic self-definition.[20] Lovett writes:

". . . authentic Pentecostal encounter cannot occur unless liberation becomes the consequence. It is another way of saying no man can experience the fullness of the Spirit and be a racist."[21]

Thirdly, white Pentecostalism is racist in an institutional sense. The superiority of whites over Blacks is promoted by Pentecostalism in several ways. There is segregation in the organizations and their wider alliances. Whites have fled the inner cities and have often sold their properties for a handsome profit. Those congregations which remain are often securely under white control. Blacks are relegated to subordinate positions, the image of Christ is white and the illustrations used in Sunday School literature are all white. The same may be said regarding the "haves" and the "have nots." White Pentecostalism is anti-Third World as well. It traces its lineage back to the Wesleys, Luther, and even to Palestine, but there is no place for Africanity in it.[22]

We now look briefly at the critique of Pentecostalism by Black theology with social consciousness in view. Theological spokespersons for the Black Pentecostals see the need for the social

---

19. *Ibid.* p. 41.

20. Tinney, *Op. Cit.* Cf. his article, "William J. Seymour: Father of Modern-Day Pentecostalism, *Journal of Religious Thought* (Vol. IV, No. 1, 1976) pp. 34-44.

21. Lovett, *Op. Cit.* p. 48.

22. Tinney, "Exclusivist Tendencies, etc. *op. cit.* p. 45.

outreach aspect of the Gospel. The Spirit descends like a Dove, but He also comes as Wind and Fire to liberate from oppressed conditions like racism and poverty.

Bennie Goodwin is even more forceful and to the point:

"The times in which we live demand more than people jumping around in a church, lifting their hands and saying, 'Praise the Lord' in an unknown tongue. The times demand that we speak with power to the powerful in a known tongue. The times demand that we discover where the power is trying to express itself in us, and that we develop that expresion. We must take our places among the powerful and devote the God-given Pentecostal power within us to the liberation of the poor, the broken-hearted, the oppressed, the blind and the bruised."[23]

In essence, then, Black Pentecostals have called attention to the racism which has splintered the Pentecostal ranks. It has provided a very perceptive critique of the authenticity of the fellowship, theology and practice of white Pentecostalism. The "fruits of the Spirit" are absent in regard to the humanity of Blacks and the poor. What can we say concerning the source of such Pentecostal manifestation? With all of its fervent claims to the outpouring of the Spirit in the individual soul, there is so little evidence of concerns for making life more human for the oppressed. Usually where there is oppression based upon race and class, sexism is in the wings. It appears that the critique of this movement by Black theologians may be a service to the entire church after all.

VI. *The Spirit and the Church*

We are now prepared to look at the Black church in "the power of the Spirit." We began our discussion on this subject by indicating how central a place the Spirit has in the Black church tradition. This alone justifies the Black theologian's reflection upon the doctrine of the Holy Spirit. The virtual neglect of this doctrine in works by Black theologians thus far makes the task urgent as we have noted.

There needs to be a serious development, theologically speaking, of many of the insights of the Black Pentecostal scholars by all of us. The spirit has had expression in a powerful way in most Black denominations. It would be valuable to trace the African roots of Pentecostalism among Blacks as well as the obvious universal impact of modern Black Pentecostal expression.[24] But the place to begin has to be in the primitive Christian Church and the witness of the Spirit in the whole Church of Christ.

23. See Goodwin, *Op. Cit.*
24. Tinney, "Exclusivist Tendencies, etc." *op. cit.* pp. 32-48.

The church as a creation of the Spirit is both an institution and a community. Institutions belong to the world of structures. Communities belong to the world of persons. The church as institute and community is interrelated. The church is *Event* and *Institute*. *Institute* refers to established relationships and patterns of historical and social order—stable forms and definite structures. *Event* points to the energizing of the church by the Spirit, the spontaneous quality of the human response and the character of the community's life of grace. The *Event* is foundational. The institutional elements are the result and the vessel for the event. Berkhof states the case well:

"This institutional element and the community element are related to one another as root and fruit. The root is prior to the fruit, but the fruit is the end as the root is the base. The metaphor is valid also insofar as the fruit comes and vanishes and the root is the basic and remaining element, thanks to which new fruits grow again and again."[25]

The church, the Spirit and Christ are interrelated as follows:

"In Word, sacraments and ministry, Christ is made present to the community of his church. This community in its turn is called to be the means by which Christ is made present to the world . . . The institute is not the first root—that is Christ himself. And the community is not the last aim—that is humankind as a whole. So the Spirit draws wider and wider the circles around Christ. The church is somewhere in the middle between Christ and the universe, as a partial realization of his goal and as a representative of his deeds and purposes toward the world. The unity of these two aspects is the nature of the church."[26]

The Black church tradition illustrates the relation of the church as event to the church as institute. The Black church is operating in the power of the Spirit which moves from worship to social involvement, as it has frequently done throughout its history. Major Jones is perceptive as he writes concerning the church as "event." He sees the gathered church as event, but he does not establish a proper connection between the church as event and institute. This, I believe, is why he also has a problem providing a theological basis for his ethics and ends up with "an ethic of distress." Just as the "event church" comes and goes, even so a Christian, when faced with tough moral choices, does not take his faith into action. One leaves his/her faith by the way, according to Jones, does what has to be done, and then returns to reclaim one's faith.[27] M. L. King, Jr., in my judgment, moved from the church as event to the church as institute. His theology was the foundation for his social activism. This we may assert without agreeing com-

25. Berkhof, *Op. Cit.*, p. 63.

26. *Ibid.*, pp. 64-65.

27. *Black Awareness: A Theology of Hope* (Nashville: Abingdon, 1971), pp. 57-58; 100-101.

pletely with either King's ethics or theology. It is consistent with the Black church tradition to assert that the same Spirit which is present when the community is "gathered" also sends Black Christians forth to claim their humanity. The spirit that comforts and heals in Black worship, renews and empowers us as we oppose the evils in the society which would humiliate and destroy us.

Moltmann's explorations into what he calls "a messianic ecclesiology" asserts that the church as a messianic fellowship depends upon the presence and power of the Holy Spirit. He writes:

"The church is a means of salvation, through proclamation, baptism, the Lord's Supper, worship, prayer, acts of blessing and the center for individual comfort and corporate fellowship. But, on the other hand, the church consists of *chrismata*, ministries, gifts and tasks which flow from this fellowship into society. These 'means of salvation' and these ministries are for the purpose of the role of the church as a messianic fellowship in the world . . . a messianic fellowship of service for the Kingdom of God."[28]

Black Christians have always been concerned about the relation of the Spirit's presence and power to what happens between persons and not merely with what happens inside of us. We have perceived that the Holy Spirit of God seems to have the greatest interest in relationships between human beings. The Beatitudes and reference to "the fruits of the Spirit" in Galatians 5 have been clearly in mind as inherent in the Gospel and as an indication of the spirit's presence and power. Even where "the second blessing" is important, social justice is sought also. In the words of Samuel Rayan:

"The Holy Spirit is in truth the Father of the poor, the one who is really concerned with the less fortunate and the marginated."[29]

We began our discussion on the Holy Spirit by noting how important the Spirit's presence and power is in the Black church tradition. We indicated that a serious discussion of the Holy Spirit by Black theologians is overdue. We then attempted to offer a working definition of the Holy Spirit. We found that it was essential to relate Christology to our discussion on the Holy Spirit. Christ, we noted, both bears and sends the Spirit. When the Spirit is examined to determine its source, we understand the Holy Spirit in concert with the revelation of God in Jesus Christ. We looked at the claims of Pentecostals regarding the Second Blessing and questioned the authenticity of this in view of the "gifts" which the Spirit bestows upon all Christians to minister in Christ's name. Black Pentecostals, we observed, have made telling criticism of the

---

28. Jurgen Moltmann, *The Church in the Power of the Spirit* (New York: Harper and Row, 1975), p. 198.

29. *The Holy Spirit* (Maryknoll, NY: Orbis, 1978), p. 137.

privileged, exclusive and racist character of white Pentecostalism. We found their observations helpful in pointing to the manner in which Blacks understand the presence and power of the Spirit. The Spirit not only heals. The Spirit empowers for liberation from oppression. Finally, we saw the church as *event* and *institute*. The spirit-filled community, the Family of God, is empowered for a messianic witness and ministry to hasten the coming of God's Kingdom. In sum, in the Black church tradition, the Spirit is not merely a Dove, but Wind and Fire also. The Comforter is also the Strengthener. Justice in the social order, no less than joy and peace in the hearts of believers, is for the Black church evidence of the Spirit's presence and power.

TOWARD A COMMON EXPRESSION OF FAITH: A BLACK NORTH AMERICAN PERSPECTIVE

Introduction

A special consultation on one common expression of the Apostolic faith from the perspective of Black Christians in the U.S. brought together representatives of several Black denominations at Virginia Union University in Richmond, Virginia, December 14-15, 1984. The consultation included representatives of the Black constituencies of several predominantly white denominations. In some cases the participants were delegated by denominational administrative headquarters; others were representatives of their communions without official appointment. The content of this document, therefore, stands upon the authority of the consultation alone and does not purport to convey the agreements of an ecclesiastical council of Black churches.

This document, moreover, does not pretend to be an exhaustive response to the Apostolic Faith Study or a formal statement of the major themes of the Black theology movement that has evolved in North America in recent years. The Richmond Consultatión, sponsored by the Commission on Faith and Order of the National Council of Churches in the U.S.A., attempted to convey to the World Council of Churches and to other interested organizations what we, a group of Black theologians and church leaders from across the United States, perceive as a general consensus among us concerning a common expression of the faith of the One, Holy, Catholic and Apostolic Church. In the several working papers we discussed and in this report we seek to add to the worldwide ecumenical study of a common expression of apostolic faith the distinctive perceptions and insights that come out of the historic experience of Black Christians in North America.

As Black academics, denominational officials, pastors and lay leaders, we speak out of more than two hundred years of suffering and struggle as "the stepchildren of church history" who have been ridiculed, ignored and scored by the white churches of both

---

"The Gift of Blackness" by Cornish Rogers (*Christian Century*, June 5-12, 1985) provides an account of the Black Churches Consultation held at Virginia Union University, Richmond, Virginia on December 14, 15, 1984.

Europe and North America. The truth of the Gospel among our people, that some have sought to suppress or disregard, burns like fire in our bones. In any discussion of one common expression of faith we have no alternative other than to make certain clear affirmations to those churches that directly or indirectly participated in and benefited from the rape of Africa that resulted in the exploitation and oppression of an African Diaspora wherever Black people are found.

We speak, however, from our own particular locus in the so-called First World, where we are less than twelve percent of the population of what is the richest and most powerful nation in the world. But inasmuch as our churches and people have never truly shared that wealth and power, we speak as a marginated Black community with a unique understanding of white racism and with strong affinities with the so-called Third World.

In this document, from an historic consultation in Richmond, Virginia, we make bold to declare that God, our Creator, has condescended through Jesus Christ, our Liberator, by the power of the Holy Spirit, our Advocate and Comforter, to convey, preserve and enhance the faith of the Apostles among the despised and alienated African American people of the United States. We commend to all who may be concerned the fruit of our prayerful reflection on the themes of the unity, holiness, catholicity and apostolicity of the Church of Jesus Christ as we join with you in search of a common expression of the faith.

I. UNITY

We affirm that the unity of the Church not only expresses the unity of the Triune God, but is also a sign of the unity of humankind that holds together in one family the diversity of all races and cultures. In the economy of God each "tribe", each ethnic group and culture has its own vocation to bring its gift to the full household of faith. Notwithstanding the effort of some white Christians to disdain the contribution of Black folk to the faith and to its impact upon the institutions of the American church and society, we declare that the meaning of Blackness as cultural and religious experience edifies and enriches the universal message of the Christian faith. Blackness, in the religions of the African Diaspora, is a profound and complex symbol of a diversified yet united experience: servitude and oppression, faithfulness through suffering, identification with the exclusion, martyrdom and exaltation of Jesus as the Oppressed One of God who triumphs over enemies, a passion for justice and liberation, the exuberance of Black faith and life, rejoicing in the Risen Lord in Pentecostal fervor and in service to the "least" of Christ's brothers and sisters.

White Christians have too often treated unity as if it were only a spiritual reality. We believe that unity must not be spiritualized, but manifested in concrete behavior, by doing just and loving service to one another. The cost of unity in the Church is repentance and affirmative discipleship (i.e., action). We have, therefore, a profound hermeneutical suspicion about any movement for unity that is dominated by North Atlantic attitudes and assumptions. We have observed that when our white brothers and sisters speak of unity they often mean being together on terms that carefully maintain their political, economic and cultural hegemony. Unity is frequently confused with "Anglo-conformity"—strict adherence to premises and perspectives based upon the worldview and ethos of the North Atlantic community with its history of racial oppression. Christian unity is, however, based upon the worship of a common Creator who is no respecter of persons, obedience to a common Lawgiver and Judge whose commandment to break every yoke is not abrogated by the gracious justification of sinners, and upon participation in the earthly mission of a common Redeemer, the sharing of whose suffering and ordeal makes us truly one, though of many races and cultures.

Blackness is one of God's gifts for the realization of the unity of the Church and humankind at this critical stage of history. It has been preserved by God as a cultural and religious inheritance of the Black churches of Africa, the Caribbean, and North and South American since the mission of the Ethiopian eunuch to the upper Nile Valley after his baptism by the Evangelist. It is rooted in the divine revelation to our African ancestors who lived before the Christian era. It has traditionally celebrated the goodness of the Almighty Sovereign God and the goodness of creation. It has emphasized the humanity of the historical Jesus, i.e., his earthly life, example, teaching, suffering, death and resurrection. It confesses belief in the humanity of Jesus together with the oneness with God, the Creator, and the Holy Spirit, but understands that humanity in non-sexist terms rather than being exclusively of the male gender. It identifies with the shadow of death that falls upon the Cross as a symbol of suffering and shame, yet crowned with light inexpressible in the victory of the resurrection.

Thus, the meaning of unity is related to the meaning of Blackness for the Afro-American Church and points to its vocation as a church of the poor and oppressed who claim liberation in the Black Messiah of God and want to share the humanizing experience of suffering and joy in struggle with others who want to work for a world of justice and equality for all. Unity is possible only when there is acceptance of suffering under Christ's work of liberation and when there is commitment to his mission.

II. HOLINESS

The Black churches of North America made a unique contribution to the Holiness and Pentecostal movements of world Christianity at the beginning of this century. The Black Pentecostal obsession with the text of Hebrews 12:14 "strive . . . for the holiness without which no one will see the Lord" (RSV), and Black leadership of the interracial Azusa Street Revival of 1906-1908 in Los Angeles created the groundwork for modern pentecostalism—the most remarkable religious movement among the oppressed communities of the world since the Awakenings of the 18th and 19th centuries. Although most African American churches did not originate from pentecostalism or the Azusa Street Revival, most of them have been influenced by the Pentecostal emphasis upon the *ruach/pneuma* of God in their conception of the Person and Work of the Holy Ghost. Their understanding of holiness as a process of moral perfection is rooted in the necessity of a personal encounter with God that is manifested in both the ecstasy of congregational worship and the praxis of social justice.

Afro-American spirituality has to do with self-transcendence and is unembarrassed by displays of sincere emotion, but it is also related to faith and action in the world. The Holy Spirit moves, therefore, in the real world of everyday life, in the sanctuary and the realm of secular affairs. The Holy Spirit is not an abstraction of Trinitarian theology but participates dynamically in what it means to be a human being and to suffer and struggle with the assurance of victory in this world as in the world to come. The distinctiveness of the Black religious experience is that theology is experienced before it is thought. Moreover, holiness in the paradoxical sense of transcendence and existential involvement in the world must accompany the act of "doing theology". Holiness is a criterion of the Church's theological authenticity. It creates a theology that is "hummed, sung and shouted" in Black churches, and contrary to white fundamentalism, has more to do with how Christians treat one another than how strictly they hold to biblical literalism or ascetic lifestyles.

On the other hand, holiness in the Black Church is not coterminous, as in some expressions of white liberalism, with frenetic social activism. Personal encounter with God as a prerequisite of sanctification and commitment to social transformation are both necessary, but the obligation to "give glory to God," to "glorify the holiness of God" is an essential corollary of the obligation to be engaged in "building the Kingdom" that continues to be frustrated by racism and oppression. The Black Church is sustained by prayer and praise. It exists in and for the glory of God and not the glorification of human institutions. We know that to struggle in the midst of the world is to experience the glory of God that is thwarted by racism and oppression, but we also know that we need to praise God in the sanctuary in order to struggle! One of our spirituals has the refrain: "Have you got good religion?" The response is, "Certainly, certainly, certainly Lord!" *Good* religion is, therefore, understood to make worldly things that were formerly dubious better, and *bad* religion ruins the best of all possible worlds where there is no acknowledgement of God's presence. Without holiness no one shall see the Lord.

Ultimately, the holiness of the Church is a work of the Holy Spirit. We affirm that the One, Holy Church cannot exist apart from ministries of justice and liberation. We also affirm that true liberation is inseparable from deep spirituality. The intimate involvement of Christians with the Holy Spirit is expressed first in worship that celebrates the manifest presence, goodness and glory of God and moves from the sanctuary to the streets where it empowers the world to goodness, transfigures its wretchedness and need, and creates the quality of life that is symbolized by the nimbus that encircles the throne of God.

III. CATHOLICITY

Although Afro-American Christians have customarily been denied equal partnership in the *koinonia* of Christ, we nevertheless affirm the universality of the Christian faith. Universality in the Black religious experience has to do with the particular reality of people in concrete situations that are dissimilar but inseparable. Afro-American churches share with all who confess Jesus Christ the conviction of the universality of God's love "from each to all in every place. . .". We recognize solidarity in creation, sin and redemption with all human beings and seek with them to make catholicity visible by overcoming humanly erected barriers between people.

We deplore the fact that the profession of universality has actually meant that the norms of what is considered acceptable to the Church had to originate in the West. For years anything that white Christians in Europe and North America did not interpret as catholic lay outside the realm of true faith and proper order. Such assumptions distorted the truth about Jesus Christ and permitted the Gospel to be used to divide people rather than free them to express the fullness of the faith in their own cultural styles and traditions. It also robbed the white churches of the opportunity to correct their own deficiencies.

In the late 18th and early 19th centuries, Black preachers were refused ordination and their congregations were not considered in good order. Not until rebellious white Methodist and separatist Baptist clergy defined custom and accepted them as duly constituted ministers and churches did Black Christianity become legitimate in the eys of Whites. To this day Black churches have protested any semblance of alienation or exclusion on account of race, class or discriminatory educational qualifications. Unfortunately the struggle for sexual equality has lagged behind in many Black churches and Black women need greater support in their resistance to subordination.

From the perspective of the Richmond consultation, catholicity has to do with faith in Jesus Christ, baptism, and continuing in "the apostles' teaching and fellowship" and in "the breaking of bread and the prayers" (Acts 2:42). No person, group or institution that meets these requirements should be excluded from the visible Church or relegated to an inferior status by human authority, ecclesiastical or secular. The sin of racism, sexism and classism that refuses or discourages the fellowship of African Independent church or Black Holiness and Pentecostal denominations, among others in various parts of the world, must be repudiated as denying the catholicity of the Body of Christ.

Catholicity, in our view, also demands a persistent critique of and challenge to the economic and political status quo; for those churches that benefit from the existing international order too easily assume its normative character and become self-appointed guardians of what is supposedly good for all. Thus, many North American conservatives and fundamentalists speak of American democracy as "Christian" and oppose Christian socialists as irregular at best and heretical at worst. Similarly, the "Moral Majority" in the U.S. supports "constructive engagement" with apartheid in South Africa as consistent with universal reason and the welfare of "all people of good will". In this view anti-communism becomes the test of universal Christian ethics and those who do not fall into line are considered sectarian, ignorant and contrary to the mainstream white American tradition which is regarded as the universal faith of the Church.

Jesus Christ challenged the assumption that faith in God or salvation was limited to the scribes and the Pharisees, or the rich and powerful. Instead he empowered sinners, the poor, strangers and women. His demonstration of catholicity was to open his arms to all who would be saved. His Church today can do no more or less.

IV. APOSTOLICITY

We affirm the Apostolic tradition that recognizes the transmission of authentic faith down the centuries by all those who have faithfully lived it, whether or not they have been officially designated as apostles. We believe that, "What does not teach Christ is not Apostolic, even if it was taught by Peter or Paul; again what preaches Christ, this is Apostolic, even when preached by

Judas, Annas, Pilate and Herod.'' We recognize, therefore, the apostolicity of what we have received from our slave ancestors who, though "unlearned and ignorant" men and women, reinterpreted the distorted Christianity they received from the slavemasters and passed down to succeeding generations of Black believers the story of Jesus who was "the strong Deliverer", "the rose of Sharon, the bright and morning star", "the king who rides on a milk-white horse", "the dying lamb", "the Lord who's done just what he said", "the Balm in Gilead", and "the help of the poor and needy, in this lan' . . .''. But we acknowledge the importance of the Apostolic tradition being engaged and not merely passed on. Apostolicity must be lived out in the context of contemporary events. It is not the recitation of past formulations, but the living of the present commandments of the Risen Lord.

In the final analysis the test of apostolicity is the experiencing of the life, death and resurrection of Jesus Christ in our daily struggle against demonic powers that seek to rob us of our inheritance as children of God redeemed by the blood of Jesus Christ. Our deeds, more than our creeds, determine whether we have fully received and acted upon the faith of the apostles.

Jesus said, "If you continue in my word, you are truly my disciples, and you will know the truth, and the truth will make you free" (John 8:31, 32). Afro-American Christians look to the words and acts of the Jesus of history for the Apostolic teaching as well as to the mystery of the Christ of faith. We take seriously the life, ministry and teaching of Jesus as the One who identified with the marginated of society and continues to identify with them. It is in the Black Church's historic identification with marginality that Jesus is appropriated as the Black Messiah, the paradigm of our existential reality as an oppressed people and the affirmation of our survival and liberation.

Finally, for Black Christians, the search for an expression of the Apostolic faith must be multiracial and multicultural rather than captive to anyone race, sex, class or political ideology. The Church and the ecumenical movement must no longer submit to domination by social, economic or intellectual elites. The faith once delivered to the apostles by Jesus Christ is for the whole world and must be capable of being transmitted and responded to by all.

CONCLUSION AND RECOMMENDATIONS

1. The Afro-American Christian tradition, embodied particulary in Black Baptist, Methodist and Pentecostal Churches, but continuing also in other Black-led Protestant and Roman Catholic congregations, has been and continues to be an indigenous expression of the faith of the apostles in North America.

2. The Richmond Consultation affirms the World Council of Churches study "Towards the Common Expression of the Apostolic Faith Today" and is committed to work with the WCC and other ecumenical bodies toward the unity we seek.
3. We invite the other churches participating in the Faith and Order movement to give greater study and recognition to how God has maintained the continuity of the Apostolic Faith primarily through the oral character and noncreedal styles of the African American tradition expressed in worship, witness and social struggle.
4. We urge the other member churches of the National and World Council Commissions on Faith and Order to take note of the unity of faith and practice that the Black Church has historically emphasized and to engage the Faith and Order movement in greater involvement in the struggle against racism and all forms of oppression as an essential element of the Apostolic confession.
5. We call upon Black churches in North and South America, the Caribbean and in Africa to confess boldly the faith we received from the Apostles, despite every effort made to distort and falsify it and, joining with us who were a part of this historic consultation in Richmond, to intensify their involvement in the Faith and Order movement by sharing the "gift of Blackness" with those of other traditions.
6. Finally, we urge that this report be published and widely disseminated by the Commission on Faith and Order of the WCC as a study document and that Black Christians all over the world be encouraged to initiate interracial discussion groups for the consideration of its content and implications for the ecumenical movement; and that the result of such dissemination and discussion be reported back to the Commission on Faith and Order by cooperating national councils.

Co-Chairs of the Consultation: David Shannon and Gayraud Wilmore.

PARTICIPANTS: Vinton Anderson, John Brandon, Oree Broomfield, Herbert Edwards, Willie Dell, Jacqueline Grant, Vincent Harris, Thomas Hoyt, Donald Jacobs, Miles Jones, John Kinney, Craig Lewis, Leonard Lovett, Fred Massey, Deborah McGill-Jackson, Pearl McNeil, Henry Mitchell, Ella Mitchell, C.J. Malloy, Albert Pero, Channing Phillips, Herbert Plummer, James DeOtis Roberts, Cornish Rogers, A.M. Spaulding, Olivia Stokes, Darius Swann, Robert Taylor, Richard Thompson, John Satterwhite. Commission on Faith and Order: Jeffrey Gros and William Rusch.

"WHAT WE HAVE SEEN AND HEARD"

BLACK BISHOPS PASTORAL ON EVANGELIZATION

In a letter issued on September 9, 1984, the ten Black U.S. bishops in the Roman Catholic Church address the concerns of racism as the major impediment to evangelization within the Black community.

INTRODUCTION

(Cf. Pope Paul VI, apostolic exhortation "Evangelii Nuntiandi," 1, 6-12, 14-16, 17, 20-24, 26-27, 49-58, 75.)

Within the history of every Christian community there comes the time when it reaches adulthood. This maturity brings with it the duty, the privilege and the joy to share with others the rich experience of the "word of life." Always conscious of the need to hear the word and ever ready to listen to its proclamation, the mature Christian community feels the irresistible urge to speak that word:

"This is what we proclaim to you: what was from the beginning, what we have heard, what we have seen with our eyes, what we have looked upon and our hands have touched—we speak the word of life. (This life became visible; we have seen and bear witness to it, and we proclaim to you the eternal life that was present to the Father and became visible to us.) What we have seen and heard we proclaim in turn to you so that you may share life with us. This fellowship of ours is with the Father and with his Son, Jesus Christ. Indeed, our purpose in writing you this is that our joy may be complete" (I Jn. 1:1-4).

We, the 10 black bishops of the United States, chosen from among you to serve the people of God, are a significant sign among many other signs that the Black Catholic community in the American church has now come of age. We write to you as brothers that "you may share life with us." We write also to all those who by their faith make up the people of God in the United States that "our joy may be complete." And what is this joy? It is that joy that the Ethiopian eunuch, the treasurer of the African queen, expressed in the Book of Acts when he was baptized by the deacon, Philip: He "went on his way rejoicing" (Acts 8:39). We rejoice because, like this African court official, we, the descendants of Africans brought to these shores, are now called to share our faith and to demonstrate our witness to our risen Lord.

71

We write to you, Black brothers and sisters, because each one of us is called to a special task. The Holy Spirit now calls us all to the work of evangelization. As he did for Peter, the Lord Jesus has prayed for us that our faith might not fail (Lk. 22:32), and with Paul we all are compelled to confess: "Yet preaching the Gospel is not the subject of a boast; I am under compulsion and have no choice. I am ruined if I do not preach it!" (I Cor. 9:16).

Evangelization is both a call and a response. It is the call of Jesus reverberating down the centuries: "Go into the whole world and proclaim the good news to all creation" (Mk. 16:15). The response is, "Conduct yourselves, then, in a way worthy of the Gospel of Christ" (Phil. 1:27). Evangelization means not only preaching but witnessing; not only conversion but renewal; not only entry into the community but the building up of the community; not only hearing the word but sharing it. Evangelization, said Pope Paul VI, "is a question not only of preaching the Gospel in ever wider geographic areas or to ever greater numbers of people, but also of affecting and as it were upsetting, through the power of the Gospel, mankind's criteria of judgment, determining values, points of interest, lines of thought, sources of inspiration and models of life, which are in contrast with the word of God and the plan of salvation."[1]

Pope Paul VI issued that call to the peoples of Africa when he said to them at Kampala in Uganda, "You are now missionaries to yourselves." Pope Paul also laid out for all sons and daughters of Africa the nature of the response, "You must now give your gifts of blackness to the whole church."[2]

We believe that these solemn words of our Holy Father Paul VI were addressed not only to Africans today but also to us, the children of the Africans of yesterday. We believe that the Holy Father has laid a challenge before us to share the gift of our blackness with the church in the United States. This is a challenge to be evangelizers, and so we want to write about this gift, which is also a challenge. First, we shall write about the gifts we share, gifts rooted in our African heritage. Then we will write about the obstacles to evangelization that we must still seek to overcome.

---

1. Pope Paul VI, "On Evangelization in the Modern World," 19.

2. The actual words of Pope Paul VI are the following:

"If you are able to avoid the possible dangers of religious pluralism, the danger of making your Christian profession into a kind of local folklore, or into exclusivist racism, or into egoistic tribalism or arbitrary separatism, then you will be able to remain sincerely African even in your own interpretation of the Christian life; you will be able to formulate Catholicism in terms congenial to your own culture; you will be capable of bringing to the Catholic Church the precious and original contribution of 'negritude,' which she needs particularly in this historic hour." "To the Heart of Africa" (Address to the Bishops of the African Continent at the Closing Session of a Symposium Held in Kampala, Uganda), *The Pope Speaks*, vol. 14 (1969), p. 219.

Graceful Remembrance for Our Own Evangelization

(Cf. "Evangelii Nuntiandi," 59, 68-69, 71.)

Before we go on, however, we must at the beginning remember those who brought us to new birth within the faith. When we as Black Catholics speak of missionaries, we shall never forget the devoted service that many white priests, vowed religious and laypersons gave to us as a people and still give to us daily. We shall remember and never forget that this ministry was often given at great personal sacrifice and hardship. The same holds true today.

We remember especially that those of us who have grown up in the faith owe this faith to the Black men and women who have gone before us strong in the faith and steadfast in their personal conviction. If we have reached adulthood in the fullness of the age of Christ, it is most of all thanks to our fathers and mothers and all our ancestors who kept alive an unflagging commitment to Christ and to his church throughout bitter days of slavery and the troubled times of racial segregation. Their faith was passed on to us despite the peculiar structures of racism and bondage that marred the Catholic Church in America in an earlier time.

I. THE GIFTS WE SHARE

Black Culture and Values: Informed by Faith

(Cf. "Evangelii Nuntiandi," 62-64.)

There is a richness in our Black experience that we must share with the entire people of God. These are gifts that are part of an African past. For we have heard with black ears and we have seen with black eyes and we have understood with an African heart. We thank God for the gifts of our Catholic faith, and we give thanks for the gifts of our blackness. In all humility we turn to the whole church that it might share our gifts so that "our joy may be complete."

To be Catholic is to be universal. To be universal is not to be uniform. It does mean, however, that the gifts of individuals and of particular groups become the common heritage shared by all. Just as we lay claim to the gift of blackness, so we share these gifts within the Black community at large and within the church. This will be our part in the building up of the whole church. This will also be our way of enriching ourselves. "For it is in giving that we receive."[3] Finally, it is our way to witness to our brothers and sisters within the Black community that the Catholic Church is both one and also home to us all.

---

3. From the prayer attributed to St. Francis of Assisi.

Scripture

(Cf. "Evangelii Nuntiandi," 42-43.)

African-American spirituality is based on the sacred scriptures. In the dark days of slavery, reading was forbidden, but for our ancestors the Bible was never a closed book. The stories were told and retold in sermons, spirituals and shouts. Proverbs and turns of phrase borrowed freely from the Bible. The Bible was not for our ancestors a mere record of the wonderful works of God in a bygone age; it was a present record of what was soon to come. God will lead his people from the bondage of Egypt. God will preserve his children in the midst of the fiery furnace. God's power will make the dry bones scattered on the plain snap together, and he will breathe life into them. Above all, the birth and death, the suffering and the sorrow, the burial and the resurrection tell how the story will end for all who are faithful, no matter what the present tragedy is.

For Black people the story is our story; the Bible promise is our hope. Thus when the word of scripture is proclaimed in the Black community, it is not a new message but a new challenge. Scripture is part of our roots; the Bible has sunk deep into our tradition; and the good news of the Gospel has been enmeshed in our past of oppression and pain. Still the message was heard, and we learned to celebrate in the midst of sorrow, to hope in the depths of despair and to fight for freedom in the face of all obstacles. The time has now come to take this precious heritage and to go and "tell in on the mountain."

Our Gift of Freedom

(Cf. "Evangelii Nuntiandi," 30-39.)

The good news of the Gospel is the message of liberation. "You will know the truth," said Jesus, "and the truth will set you free" (Jn. 8:32). Recently our Holy Father, Pope John Paul II, spoke at length on the relation between truth and freedom:

"Jesus himself links 'liberation' with knowledge of the truth: 'You will know the truth, and the truth will make you free' (Jn. 8:32). In this affirmation is the deep meaning of freedom that Christ gives man as a consequence coming from knowledge of the truth. It is a question of a spiritual process of maturing, by means of which man becomes a representative and spokesman of 'righteousness and holiness' (Eph. 4:24) at the different levels of personal, individual and social life. But this truth is not mere truth of a scientific or historical nature; it is Christ himself—the word incarnate of the Father—who can say of himself, 'I am the way, the truth, the life' (Jn. 14:6). For this reason, Jesus, although aware of what was in store for him, repeatedly and forcefully, with firmness and with decision, opposed 'non-truth' in his earthly life.

"This service of truth, participation in the prophetic service of Christ, is a task of the church, which tries to carry it out in the different historical contexts. It is necessary to call clearly by name injustice, the exploitation of man by man, the exploitation of man by the state or by the mechanisms of systems and regimes. It is necessary to call by name all social injustice, all discrimination, all violence inflicted on man with regard to his body, his spirit, his conscience, his dignity as a person, his life."[4]

"Let us who are the children of pain be now a bridge of reconciliation. Let us who are the offspring of violence become the channels of compassion. Let us, the sons and daughters of bondage, be the bringers of peace."

Black people know what freedom is because we remember the dehumanizing force of slavery, racist prejudice and oppression. No one can understand so well the meaning of the proclamation that Christ has set us free than those who have experienced the denial of freedom. For us, therefore, freedom is a cherished gift. For its preservation, no sacrifice is too great.

Hence, freedom brings responsibility. It must never be abused, equated with license or taken for granted. Freedom is God's gift, and we are accountable to him for our loss of it. And we are accountable for the gift of freedom in the lives of others. We oppose all oppression and all injustice, for unless all are free, none are free. Moreover, oppression by some means freedom's destruction for both the oppressor and the oppressed, and liberation liberates the oppressor and the oppressed.

Our African-American ancestors knew the liberating hand of God. Even before emancipation they knew the inner spiritual freedom that comes from Jesus. Even under slavery they found ways to celebrate that spiritual freedom which God alone can give. They left us the lesson that without spiritual freedom we cannot fight for that broader freedom which is the right of all who are brothers and sisters in Christ. This is the gift we have to share with the whole church. This is the responsibility that freedom brings: to teach to others its value and work to see that its benefits are denied to none.

The Gift of Reconciliation

(Cf. "Evangelii Nuntiandi," 2, 30-31, 61-64.)

The gospel message is a message that liberates us from hate and calls us to forgiveness and reconciliation. As a people we must

4. Pope John Paul II, "Be Witnesses to Christ, the Truth!" *You Are the Future, You Are the Hope: To the Young People of the World, John Paul II* (Daughters of St. Paul, 1979), p. 105.

be deeply committed to reconciliation. This is a value coming from our African heritage and deepened by our belief in the gospel teaching. When in recent years we rejected "token integration" for "self-determination," it was not to choose confrontation in place of cooperation, but to insist on collaboration with mutual respect for the dignity and unique gifts of all. Reconciliation can never mean unilateral elevation and another's subordination, unilateral giving and another's constant receiving, unilateral flexibility and another's resistance. True reconciliation arises only where there is mutually perceived equality. That is what is meant by justice.

Without justice, any meaningful reconciliation is impossible. Justice safeguards the rights and delineates the responsibility of all. A people must safeguard its own cultural identity and its own cultural values. Likewise it must respect the cultural values of others. For this reason sincere reconciliation builds on mutual recognition and mutual respect. On this foundation can be erected an authentic Christian love.

"But now in Christ Jesus you who once were far off have been brought near through the blood of Christ. It is he who is our peace, and who made the two of us one by breaking down the barrier of hostility that kept us apart" (Eph. 2:13-14).

We seek justice, then, because we seek reconciliation, and we seek reconciliation because by the blood of Christ we are made one. The desire for reconciliation is for us a most precious gift, for reconciliation is the fruit of liberation. Our contribution to the building up of the church in America and in the world is to be an agent of change for both.

Finally, as we speak of reconciliation, let us note that as members of a truly universal church our efforts must never be limited to the Black community in this country alone. Our minds and hearts turn toward the church of the poor in the Third World, especially those "who hunger and thirst for justice" in Africa, Asia and Latin America. We turn also to the members of the "church of silence" and to the various minority groups in the East and in the West.

We shall remind ourselves and our compatriots that we are called to be "instruments of peace." This peace is the fruit of justice. We must be a part of those movements for justice that seek to reduce bombs and increase bread, to replace bullets with the printing of books. We must work with all who strive to make available the fruits of creation to all God's children everywhere. It was in chains that our parents were brought to these shores and in violence were we maintained in bondage. Let us who are the children of pain be now a bridge of reconciliation. Let us who are the offspring of violence become the channels of compassion. Let us, the sons and daughters of bondage, be the bringers of peace.

Our Spirituality and Its Gifts

(Cf. "Evangelii Nuntiandi," 61-64.)

Black Americans are a people rich with spiritual gifts. Some aspects of this spirituality have already been mentioned. It is fitting, however, to present briefly the major characteristics of what can be termed "Black spirituality." As members of a church universal both in time and place, we have no difficulty with this term. All peoples and all cultures have been molded by the Holy Spirit, and the Holy Spirit has distributed gifts in the language, culture and traditions of each.

Black spirituality has four major characteristics: It is contemplative. It is holistic. It is joyful. It is communitarian.

The Contemplative Dimension.

Black spirituality is contemplative. By this we mean that prayer is spontaneous and pervasive in the Black tradition. Every place is a place for prayer because God's presence is heard and felt in every place. Black spirituality senses the awe of God's transcendence and the vital intimacy of his closeness. God's power breaks into the "sin-sick world' of everyday. The sense of God's presence and power taught our ancestors that no one can run from him and no one need hide from him.

Black spirituality has taught us what it means to "let go" and "to lean on God." In an age of competition and control we have learned to surrender to God's love and to let him work his power through us. In an age of technology and human engineering our spiritual heritage has never let us forget that God takes us each by the hand and leads us in ways we might not understand. It is this sense of God's power in us that calls us to work for evangelization in the modern world.

Holistic

Black spirituality, in contrast with much of Western tradition, is holistic. Like the biblical tradition, there is no dualism. Divisions between intellect and emotion, spirit and body, action and contemplation, individual and community, sacred and secular are foreign to us. In keeping with our African heritage, we are not ashamed of our emotions. For us, the religious experience is an experience of the whole human being—both the feelings and the intellect, the heart as well as the head. Moreover, we find foreign any notion that the body is evil. We find our own holistic spiritual approach to be in accord with the scriptures and the logic of the incarnation.

In sharing this approach we contribute greatly to evangelization in our day. St. Paul wrote Timothy, "Everything God created is good; nothing is to be rejected when it is received with thanksgiving" (I Tim. 4:4). The material world need not lead us away from God, but can and should bring us closer to him.

We dare to suggest that Black spirituality in its holistic approach also presents a solution to one of the problems of our time: the progressive dehumanization brought about by a technocratic society. Not only is it possible to counteract the dehumanizing forces in our world and our work, but we can restore the human. We can put back the human factor by rediscovering that "the world is charged with the grandeur of God"[5] and that "the whole world is in his hands." We affirm that the advances in technology, when understood with God's presence in all things, will be a powerful force for the coming of the kingdom and the human progress of all people.

The Gift of Joy

Joy is a hallmark of Black spirituality. Joy is first of all celebration. Celebration is movement and song, rhythm and feeling, color and sensation, exultation and thanksgiving. We celebrate the presence and the proclamation of the word.

This joy is a sign of our faith and especially our hope. It is never an escape from reality, however harsh it may be. Indeed this joy is often present even in the midst of deep anguish and bitter tears.

"You will weep and mourn while the world rejoices; you will grieve for a time, but your grief will be turned into joy." (Jn. 16:20).

This joy is a result of our conviction that "in the time of trouble, he will lead me." This joy comes from the teaching and wisdom of mothers and fathers in the faith that, looking at Jesus, we must burst forth into song so that all might hear, "He's sweet I know. . . ."

This gift of joy is something we must share. If the message of evangelization is the "good news" about Jesus, we must react with joy. If we do indeed feel a profound joy, we shall know that we have heard and that we have understood; and we are thus enabled to share our good news.

One who is joyful is impelled to love and cannot hate. A joyful person seeks to reconcile and will not cause division. A joyful person is troubled by the sight of another's sadness. A joyful person seeks to console, strives to encourage and brings to all true peace.

---

5. "God's Grandeur," *The Poems of Gerard Manley Hopkins*, 4th ed., W.H. Gardner and N.H. MacKenzie, eds. (Oxford University Press, 1970), p. 66.

Such is the gift so clearly needed in our time. Such is the gift that Jesus passed on to us on the evening he died. "All this I tell you that my joy may be yours and your joy may be complete" (Jn. 15:11).

Community

(Cf. "Evangelii Nuntiandi," 60.)

In African culture the "I" takes its meaning in the "we." In other words, individual identity is to be found within the context of the community. Even today Black Christianity is eminently a social reality. The sense of community is a major component of Black spirituality.

This communal dimension of our spirituality is also a gift we need to share. In the world in which we live, a high value is placed on competition. Hence, so many of us become "losers" so that others might prevail as "winners." And again so many place personal profit and personal advancement before the good of the community and the benefit of the whole.

The communal dimension of Black spirituality permeates our experience of liturgy and worship. Worship must be shared. Worship is always a celebration of community. No one stands in prayer alone. One prays and acts within and for the community. Each one supports, encourages and enriches the other and is in turn enriched, encouraged and supported.

Community, however, means social concern and social justice. Black spirituality never excludes concern for human suffering and other people's concerns. "As often as you did it for one of my least brothers, you did it for me" (Mt. 25:40) are the words of Christ that cut through any supposed tension between secular concerns and the sacred or between prayerful pursuits and the profane. Ours is a spiritual heritage that always embraces the total human person.

The Family

(Cf. "Evangelii Nuntiandi," 71).

The heart of the human community is the family. In our society today traditional family values are openly questioned and rejected. For many reasons the Black family has been especially assailed, despite the importance that families still have in the Black cultural and spiritual tradition.

For us the family has always meant "the extended family"—the grandparents, the uncles and aunts, the godparents, all those related by kinship or strong friendship. This rich notion of family was not only part of an African tradition but also was our own African-American experience. Child care became the responsibility of many persons, for necessity demanded that many share the labor, distribute the burden and, yes, even the joy.

In practice, the extended family often goes beyond kinship and marital relationship to include persons who, having no family of their own, have been accepted into the wider family circle. These family members feel a deep responsibility for one another in both ordinary times of daily life and in the extraordinary moments of need or crisis.

It is for this reason that, despite the erosion of family life among us, we as a people continue to have a strong sense of family bonds. In its Christian setting this family sense enhances the role of godparents and other relatives who must often shoulder the responsibility for passing on the faith and strengthening the religious values of the young. Moreover, there is more than one priestly or religious vocation among us that was nurtured by the support and encouragement of some adult in the extended family. Not infrequently young Blacks in the seminary or religious-formation house have been informally adopted by a sponsor or have been welcomed into the circle of a second family.

This sense of family in our own African-American tradition can easily be translated into a richer sense of church as a great and all-embracing family. In our parishes we should truly look upon ourselves as brothers and sisters to one another. The elders among us should be a living resource for the young, for they have much to tell and teach. Our celebrations should be the affirmation of our kinship and our common bond. The words of the third Eucharistic Prayer, "Father, hear the prayers of the family you have gathered here before you," are not a pious fiction but a sacred reality that defines the meaning of the Catholic community. In a word, evangelization for Black Catholics is a celebration of the family, a renewal of the family and a call to welcome new members into the family of God.

The Role of Black Men

(Cf. "Evangelii Nuntiandi," 73, 76.)

Central to any discussion of the Black family today is the question of the Black man as husband, father, co-provider and co-protector. For many historical reasons the Black man has been forced to bear the crushing blows of racial hate and economic repression. Too often barred from access to decent employment, too often stripped of his dignity and manhood and too often forced into a stereotype that was a caricature of his manhood, the Black male finds himself deprecated and relegated to the margins of family life and influence. Not least of the evil fruits of racial segregation has been the artifically fashioned rivalry between Black women and men.

It is important, we believe, to encourage a re-evaluation of the fundamental vocation to fatherhood that Black men must have in the context of the Black family. In our cultural heritage the father provides the courage and wisdom to help maintain the family and to ensure its growth. We challenge Black men of today to assert their spiritual strength and to demonstrate their sense of responsibility and ethnic pride. We call upon Black men to become what their fathers were—even when an evil institution sought to destroy their individuality and their initiative—that is, models of virtue for their children and partners in love and nurturing with their wives. Without a father no family life can be fully complete. Let the Black father find his model in the fatherhood of God, who by his providence nourishes us, who by his wisdom guides us and who by his love cherishes us and makes us all one and holy in his family of grace.

The Role of Black Women

(Cf. "Evangelii Nuntiandi," 73, 76.)

The civil rights movement of the 1960s that we as a people initiated and in which we suffered raised the consciousness of many people to the reality of social inequities and social injustice. In many ways our struggle served as a pattern and a model for others who were made aware of their own plight. Within the last decade we all have become more conscious of the social inequities that women as a group have suffered and continue to suffer in our society. In a very special way these inequities weigh most heavily on Black women and women of other racial minorities.

On the other hand, Black women have had and continue to have a place within the Black community that is unique. In traditional Black society women have had to assume responsibilities within the family and within the community out of necessity. As a result, Black women historically have been not only sources of strength, they also have been examples of courage and resolution. This strength and courage are for us all a source of power and a powerful gift that we as a people can share with the larger society.

The role of Black women within the context of Black history, however, has not been a subordinate role to Black men, but a complementary role. Women like Sojourner Truth, Harriet Tubman and Mary McLeod Bethune were heirs of an African tradition.

If this is true of the African-American tradition, it is even more so for us who are the heirs of a Black Catholic tradition. Before there were Black Catholic priests in the United States, there were Black women religious. The challenge of evangelization within the Black Catholic community was taken up by four Black women in the hostile environment of Baltimore, under the leadership of Elizabeth Lange. The church gave approval to her work when the Oblate Sisters of Providence were officially recognized as a religious congregation in 1831. Evangelization among the Blacks of New Orleans was also the task assumed by Henriette Delille, who in the face of crushing opposition founded the Sisters of the Holy Family in 1842. These two Black congregations of religious women were joined by a third in our own century when Mother Theodore Williams helped establish the Franciscan Handmaids of the Most Pure Heart of Mary in 1916 in Savannah, Georgia.

"In an age of technology and human engineering, our spiritual heritage has never let us forget that God takes us each by the hand and leads us in ways we might not understand. It is this sense of God's power in us that calls us to work for evangelization in the modern world."

These Black women religious leaders and the sisters whom they formed were not only witnesses of faith; they were also a sign of the faith of many Black Catholic families who, even in the dark days of slavery, gave not only support, but even their daughters and sisters in the service of the Gospel.

Within the Black Catholic community today, Black women continue to witness in various non-ordained ministries, both as religious and lay. This ministry is to be found on the parochial and the diocesan level. It is a ministry in schools and in the social apostolate. Needless to say, this potential for service within our own community needs to be more fully recognized and utilized by the Catholic Church in the United States. Black women can and should be considered as collaborators in the work of evangelization. The words of the pastoral commission of the Congregation for the Evangelization of Peoples are eminently true of women in the Black Catholic community: "Givers of life, consecrated by nature to its service, it is for women to give to evangelization a living and realistic face before the world."[6]

Abortion and Black Values

(Cf. "Evangelii Nuntiandi," 65.)

Today the Black family is assailed on all sides. Much has been said by others about the economic plight of the Black family. We would like to add a word regarding the moral aspect of this plight.

The acceptance of abortion by many as a common procedure and even as a right is a reality not only in our American society as a whole, but also within the Black community. And yet life, and especially new life within the mother, has always been a value to Africans and to African-Americans. Historically, even children conceived outside of marriage were cherished and given a place in

---

6. Pastoral Commission of the Congregation for the Evangelization of Peoples, *The Role of Women in Evangelization, Vatican II: More Postconciliar Documents*, Austin Flannery, O.P., gen. ed. (Northport, N.Y., 1982), p. 327.

the extended family. Black cultural tradition has always valued life and the mystery of its transmission and growth. Children have always been for us a sign of hope. The loss of this perspective is a cultural and spiritual impoverishment for us as a people.

From our point of view as Catholics and as Black people, we see the efforts made "to provide" low-cost abortions as another form of subjugation. Indeed there are those who would even characterize it as a form of genocide. As a people of faith, it is our task to fight for the right to life of all our children and in all the circumstances of their existence. It is our duty to reassert the gift of our traditional African-American values of family and children to our own people and to our society as a whole. It is equally our duty, however, to show practical concern and honest compassion for the many mothers-to-be who are too often encouraged to seek an abortion by the conventional wisdom of our society today.

"Our own history has taught us that preaching to the poor and to those who suffer injustice without concern for their plight . . . is to trivialize the Gospel and mock the cross."

Finally, we add this unfortunate observation: If society truly valued our children and our mothers—mothers who have already made a choice for life—they would have day-care centers, jobs, good schools and all else that a just society should offer to its people. Sadly we observe that if abortion were abolished tomorrow, the same diastrous ills would plague our Black mothers and children.

Ecumenism
(Cf. "Evangelii Nuntiandi," 39, 65-68, 77-79, 80.)

There exists a reality which is called "the Black church." It crosses denominational boundaries and is without a formal structure. Yet is is a reality cherished by many Black Christians, who feel at ease joining in prayer and in Christian action with one another. This Black church is a result of our common experience and history —it has made it possible for many Blacks to understand and appreciate each other.

This does not mean that Black people, and especially Black Catholics, are indifferent to the distinctions of various denominations. Black Catholics as well as all Black Christians are loyal to their respective faith communities. Black Catholics most particularly, whether by birth or conversion in later life, insist upon total loyalty to all that is Catholic. A deep abiding love of the Catholic Church is a characteristic of Black Catholicism.

Nevertheless, because we as a people have been a deeply religious people, as Black Catholics we are in a special position to serve as a bridge with our brothers and sisters of other Christian traditions. We wish to encourage our Black Catholics to deepen their awareness and understanding of the whole Black church, inasmuch as the majority of Black Chrisitans in this country are separated from Catholic unity.

It is to this end that Pope Paul VI called us when he stated:

"As Catholics our best ecumenical efforts are directed both to removing the causes of separation that still remain, as well as to giving adequate expression to the communion which already exists among all Christians. We are sustained and encouraged in this task because so many of the most significant elements and endowments that are Christ's gifts to his church are the common source of our strength."[7]

And, in reference to the wealth of spiritual joy and expression in the Black church, these words spoken by Pope John Paul II in New York would seem especially appropriate for us: "I wish to greet in you the rich variety of your nation, where people of different ethnic origins and creeds can live, work and prosper together in mutual respect."[8]

Finally, the following words of Pope John Paul II would seem appropriate for our relationships with our Muslim and Jewish brothers and sisters:

"Does it not sometimes happen that the firm belief of the followers of the non-Christian religions—a belief that is also an effect of the Spirit of truth operating outside the visible confines of the mystical body—can make Christians ashamed at being often themselves so disposed to doubt concerning the truths revealed by God and proclaimed by the church and so prone to relax moral principles and open the way to ethical permissiveness?"[9]

II. THE CALL OF GOD TO HIS PEOPLE

Perspective

(Cf. "Evangelii Nuntiandi," 61-62.)

If the story of America is told with honesty and clarity, we must all recognize the role that Blacks have played in the growth of this country. At every turning point of American history, we come face to face with the Black man and Black woman. What is true of our national history is even truer of American Catholic history.

---

7. Pope Paul VI, "Message to the World Council of Churches General Assembly at Nairobi," *Doing the Truth in Charity: Statements of Pope Paul VI, John Paul I, John Paul II, and the Secretariat for Promoting Christian Unity, 1964-1980* (Paulist Press, 1982), p. 291.

8. Pope John Paul II, "The Ideal of Liberty, a Moving Force," *U.S.A.: The Message of Justice, Peace and Love* (Daughters of St. Paul, 1979), p. 96.

9. Pope John Paul II, *Redemptor Hominis*, 6.

Just as the church in our history was planted by the efforts of the Spaniards, the French and the English, so did it take root among Indians, Black slaves and the various racial mixtures of them all. Blacks—whether Spanish-speaking, French-speaking or English-speaking—built the churches, tilled church lands and labored with those who labored in spreading the Gospel. From the earliest period of the church's history in our land, we have been the hands and arms that helped build the church from Baltimore to Bardstown, from New Orleans to Los Angeles, from St. Augustine to St. Louis. Too often neglected and too much betrayed, our faith was witnessed by Black voices and Black tongues—such as Jean-Baptiste Pointe du Sable, Pierre Toussaint, Elizabeth Lange, Henriette Delille and Augustus Tolton.

The historical roots of Black America and those of Catholic America are intimately intertwined. Now is the time for us who are Black Americans and Black Catholics to reclaim our roots and to shoulder the responsibilities of being both Black and Catholic.

The responsibility is both to our own people and to our own church. To the former, we owe the witness of our faith in Christ and in his body, the church. To the latter, we owe this witness of faith as well as the unstinting labor to denounce racism as a sin and to work for justice and inner renewal.

It is to this responsibility that we now address ourselves in this second half of our pastoral letter. We do so by setting forth the opportunities and challenges that lie before us as a people and as a church.

Black Initiative

(Cf. "Evangelii Nuntiandi," 62-63.)

We call upon our Black Catholic sisters and brothers to shoulder the responsibility laid upon us by our baptism into the body of Christ. This responsibility is to proclaim our faith and to take an active part in building up the church. The Second Vatican Council in its Decree on the Missionary Activity of the Church stated:

"The church has not been truly established and is not yet fully alive, nor is it a perfect sign of Christ among men, unless there exists a laity worthy of the name working along with the hierarchy. . . .

"Their main duty . . . is the witness which they are bound to bear to Christ by their life and works in the home, in their social group and in their own professional circle. . . . They must give expression to this newness of life in the social and cultural framework of their own homeland, according to their own national traditions. They must heal it and preserve it. . . . Let them also spread the faith of Christ among those with whom they live. . . . This obligation is all the more urgent, because very many men can hear of the Gospel and recognize Christ only by means of the laity who are their neighbors."[10]

The Black community in the United States for a long time has been a component of the missionary enterprise of the American church. In this sense these words from the Decree on Missionary Activity are perfectly valid for the American Black community. We are conscious of the debt of gratitude we owe to those who have served among us as home missionaries.

Yet we are also aware that we, like other African-Americans, are also descendants of slaves and freedmen. Like them we are victims of oppression and racism, and like them we are fighters for the same freedom and dignity. We likewise speak with the same accents and sing the same songs, and we are heirs of the same cultural achievements. Thus we have a privileged position to gain access to the hearts and minds of the African-American community. Hence, we have the solemn responsibility to take the lead in the church's work within the Black community.

On the other hand, we are in a position to counter the assumption which many have advanced that to become a Catholic is to abandon one's racial heritage and one's people! The Catholic Church is not a "white church" nor a "Euro-American church." It is essentially universal and hence Catholic. The Black presence within the American Catholic Church is a previous witness to the universal character of Catholicism.

The church, however, must preserve its multicultural identity. As Paul VI wrote, "Evangelization loses much of its force and effectiveness if it does not take into consideration the actual people to whom it is addressed, if it does not use their language, their signs and symbols, if it does not answer the questions they ask and if it does not have an impact on their concrete life."[11]

In our response to the invitation to evangelize, we as Black Catholics have before us several opportunities to assure the universal aspect of the American church. We can do so by permitting the Catholic Church in this country to reflect the richness of African-American history and its heritage. This is our gift to the church in the United States, this is our contribution to the building up of the universal church.

Authorization and Encouragement

(Cf. "Evangelii Nuntiandi," 67-73.)

Since African-American members of the American church are to assume the responsibility to which the church and our racial

---

10. *Ad Gentes* (Decree on the Missionary Activity of the Church), 21.
11. "On Evangelization in the Modern World," 63.

heritage call us, Black leaders in the church—clergy, religious and lay—need encouragement and the authorization to use their competencies and to develop their expertise. Unhappily we must acknowledge that the major hindrance to the full development of Black leadership within the church is still the fact of racism. The American Catholic bishops wrote in the pastoral letter on racism:

'The church . . . must be constantly attentive to the Lord's voice as he calls on his people daily not to harden their hearts (Ps. 94:8). We urge that on all levels the Catholic Church in the United States examine its conscience regarding attitudes and behavior toward Blacks, Hispanics, native Americans and Asians. We urge consideration of the evil of racism as it exists in the local church and reflection upon the means of combating it. We urge scrupulous attention at every level to ensure that minority representation goes beyond mere tokenism and involves authentic sharing in the responsibility and decision making.''[12]

These words have not had the full impact on the American church that was originally hoped. Blacks and other minorities still remain absent from many aspects of Catholic life and are only meagerly represented on the decision-making level. Inner-city schools continue to disappear, and Black vocational recruitment lacks sufficient support. In spite of the fact that Catholic schools are a principal instrument of evangelization, active evangelization is not always a high priority.

This racism, at once subtle and masked, still festers within our church as within our society. It is this racism that in our minds remains the major impediment to evangelization within our community. Some little progress has been made, but success is not yet attained. This stain of racism on the American church continues to be a source of pain and disappointment to all, both Black and white, who love it and desire it to be the bride of Christ "without stain or wrinkle" (Eph. 5:27). This stain of racism, which is so alien to the Spirit of Christ, is a scandal to many, but for us it must be the opportunity to work for the church's renewal as part of our task of evangelization. To "profess the truth in love" (Eph. 4:15) to our brothers and sisters within the faith remains for Black Catholics the first step in proclaiming the gospel message. We, like St. John the Baptist, proclaim a baptism of repentance for the forgiveness of sins, and we call on the American church to produce the fruit of repentance and not presume to tell themselves we have Abraham for our father, for we all belong to the family of God (cf. Lk. 3:1-9).

Our demand for recognition, our demand for leadership roles in the task of evangelization, is not a call for separatism but a pledge of our commitment to the church and to share in her

---

12. National Conference of Catholic Bishops, "Brothers and Sisters to Us: A Pastoral Letter on Racism," *Quest for Justice*, J. Brian Benestad and Francis J. Butler, co-eds. (U.S. Catholic conference, 1981), p. 382.

witnessing to the love of Christ. For the Christ we proclaim is he who prayed on the night before he died "that all may be one as you, Father, are in me, and I in you; I pray that they may be (one) in us, that the world may believe that you sent me" (Jn. 17:21).

Opportunities for Evangelization

There exist numerous opportunities for evangelization within the Black community. It is not our intention to enumerate all of these. We do propose, however, to point out those that in our opinion are the most important and the most essential. For some of these the Black community can and must seize the initiative. For others we need the cooperation and the encouragement of the entire American church.

Vocations to the Priesthood and Religious Life

From apostolic times, the local church called forth its ministers from within itself for the sake of evangelization. Paul and Barnabas evangelized the communities of Iconium, Lystra and Derbe. "In each church they installed presbyters and, with prayer and fasting, commended them to the Lord in whom they had put their faith" (Acts 14:23). This became the established practice: to plant the new church and draw from it the clergy and the teachers to continue the work of evangelization and nurture the growing congregation with pastoral care. In this way were the early churches of Africa evangelized in Egypt, Nubia, Ethiopia and North Africa.

Unfortunately, later missionaries did not always carry out this traditional practice. For too long the way to a fully indigenous clergy and religious was blocked by an attitude that was paternalistic and racist. It was especially through the efforts of the Holy See that the earlier practice was resumed. Beginning with Pope Benedict XV in 1919, with the encyclical *Maximum Illud*, and continuing on until the Second Vatican Council, the highest authority within the church has called in season and out of season for the creation of an indigenous clergy. This was to be done as soon as possible as part of the actual process of evangelization:

"It is not enough for the Christian people to be present and organized in a given nation. Nor is it enough for them to carry out an apostolate of good example. They are organized and present for the purpose of announcing Christ to their non-Christian fellow citizens by word and deed, and of aiding them toward the full reception of Christ.

"We cannot overemphasize the tremendous importance of parochial schools . . . The efforts made to support them and to ensure their continuation are a touchstone of the local church's sincerity in the evangelization of the Black community."

"Now, if the church is to be planted and the Christian community grow, various ministries are needed. These are raised up by divine vocation from the midst of the faithful and are to be carefully fostered and cultivated by all."[13]

If in the history of the American church many Black men and women found their vocations to the religious life and priesthood blocked by racist attitudes, this is no longer tolerable. It is now the responsibility and the duty of the Black Catholic community to encourage young men and women to follow Christ in the priesthood and in the consecrated life.

The duty lies especially with all those who have contact with youth. We call first upon the Black family to set before the eyes of the young the value of service to Christ in ministry of others, both at the altar and in the manifold areas of evangelization. Black parents will do this by passing on to their children the truths of the Catholic religion and the spiritual values of our African-American heritage. When a child shows signs of a priestly or religious vocation, the parents will respect and even encourage this sign of God's call.

We call upon teachers and educators and all those who work with youth in the Black community to be aware of this vocation when it appears among Black youth. Let them not underestimate their influence for good regarding the young. Let them never belittle or discourage the manifestation of the Spirit. Moreover, let them encourage those more mature men and women who, touched by grace, follow a religious vocation as a second career.

Most particularly we remind our Black sisters and brothers who have already answered God's call that they especially have the task to foster Black vocations. All young people crave role models. Black sisters, brothers and priests must be such models for Black youth today. Let them take care to be always a positive influence. If in their own lives of service they have had to struggle because of racial discrimination, let them now be beacons of hope for those who follow after. Even if in their own lives they have experienced the contradictions of a racist society, let them show forth the joy that comes to those who leave all to follow the crucified king.

In this matter of vocations, so crucial to the cause of evangelization in the Black community, we need the collaboration of the entire American church. In fact, we suggest that the recruitment of minority youth for the priesthood and religious life must have the highest priority. More precisely, let diocesan vocation directors collaborate with leaders in the Black Catholic community in strategic planning for the recruitment of Black young men for the diocesan priesthood. The same planning and collaborative effort should be part of the vocational planning of the many religious congregations and seminaries. Care should be taken to

---

13. *Ad Gentes*, 15.

know and understand the attitudes and concerns of Black young people in order to show how ministry would be relevant to their lives and experience. Above all, it is necessary for those engaged in recruitment programs, whether for the diocesan clergy or for religious life, to go where Black young people are found. It means visits to inner-city schools and the use of vocational materials that portray Blacks, Hispanics, Asians and other racial or ethnic groups.

Regretfully, experience has shown that once inside a seminary, a novitiate or a house of formation many minority students face a period of cultural and social alienation. Here again, collaborative effort is needed between seminary and formation leaders on the one hand and the minority community on the other. In the case of Black students this means helping the student to maintain contact with the Black community and to renew contact with Black culture, Black history and Black theological studies. The National Conference of Catholic Bishops called for this in 1981:

"Students who come from diverse racial and cultural backgrounds should participate in programs and adopt a pattern of life geared to ready them for pastoral responsibility among their respective peoples and to intensify their own sense of ethnic identity. . . .

"Seminarians from various ethnic groups need to maintain and develop their identity with both family and community. This will require special sensitivity on the part of those responsible for administration and formation."[14]

Not only Blacks, but all who would work in and with the Black community must understand the history, values, culture and ethos of the Black community. The American bishops call for this in the same document.

"The seminary should include in its program of studies courses presenting the history and the development of the cultural heritage of Black, Hispanic and native Americans, and other cultural and ethnic groups within the United States. Moreover, opportunities for intercultural contacts should be offered to enable future ministers to become more aware, through workshops, seminars and special sessions, of the positive values offered by other cultures. . . . Such an experience is imperative for those whose ministry, because of the ethnic population of their region, will bring them into contact with large numbers of certain racial and cultural groups. . . .

"The seminary course in church history should also include a treatment of the church's relationship to these various ethnic groups to give an insight into present difficulties facing the church in her ministry to minority groups in the United States today."[15]

---

14. National Conference of Catholic Bishops, *The Program of Priestly Formation*, 3rd ed., nos. 531, 534, 535.

15. *Ibid.*, 531, 533.

Finally, we believe it important that Black men and women be encouraged to follow the Spirit in every sector of the church. This will include the strictly contemplative orders as well. It is our profound conviction that the Holy Spirit is working among us as a people and will continue to work to bring forth fruits of holiness and prayer.

Permanent Deacons

It is a sign of the times that the Second Vatican Council in its wisdom called for the restoration of the permanent order of deacons. In the Black community this unique calling is of special importance because it provides an opportunity for men of competence who have had an experience of life much broader than that of many priests and religious. Even after ordination, many permanent deacons continue to pursue their occupation in the workaday world and in family life. This gives them access to opportunities for evangelization in places where a priest or religious might find entry difficult. This is particulary true for Black deacons in the Black community, where many of the clergy are not Black. The permanent diaconate provides an opportunity to utilize those men who are natural leaders. Furthermore, it makes use of an institution that is familiar to most Blacks, since deacons are part of the congregation in many Black Christian communities.

The permanent diaconate sacramentalizes this reality which is already present and gives it a prestige which cannot but redound to the advantage of the church in proclaiming the good news to the whole community. Incorporated into the hierarchy through the sacrament of orders and yet part of the community in whose life he shares, the Black deacon has a role of mediator which is truly unique.

Every effort should be made to recruit qualified candidates for the office of deacon from within every Black parish. All members of the parish community should be involved. Pastors should actively strive to identify and recuit likely candidates. Those who feel the desire to serve in this way should prayerfully and assiduously pursue their call. All members of the parish can make an invaluable contribution by searching out candidates and giving them encouragement and support.

What we have said regarding the formation of Black priests and religious applies to that of deacons as well. If anything, it is even more important. The deacon is called for service not only in the parish, but also at times in the diocese at large. This service demands the acquisition of those skills necessary for effective ministry. The Black deacon especially must synthesize in his life and in his understanding not only faith, but also his cultural and racial heritage. We call upon those responsible for the deacon's training and formation to prepare him for this unique task.

The Laity

(Cf. "Evangelii Nuntiandi," 24, 38, 41, 54.)

The work of evangelization is not confined to the clergy and the religious alone. It is also the responsibility of the laity. "Incorporated into Christ's mystical body through baptism and strengthened by the power of the Holy Spirit through confirmation, they are assigned to the apostolate by the Lord himself."[16]

Within the tradition of the Black community, laypersons in the Black church have always had important roles. Within the history of the Black Catholic community, at a time when the Black clergy were few, many laypersons provided leadership. We need only mention Daniel Rudd and the Black lay Catholic congresses in the 19th century and Thomas Wyatt Turner and the Federated Colored Catholics in the period prior to the Second World War.

The role of the laity needs to be better understood by both the clergy and the laity themselves. In many instances this will require study and reflection, and in some cases a change in attitude. Such understanding, moreover, is only a beginning; for if the laity are to exercise their special form of evangelization, that which is understood in theory must lead to practical plans for action and even structural change.

It is the responsibility of the clergy to facilitate, inspire and coordinate the work of the whole Christian community. This entails calling upon laywomen and laymen to join in the work of spreading the good news and authorizing and encouraging them to do so. It also means involving them in the formulation and execution of all programs leading to the building up of the body of Christ, which is the church.

Lay people in turn must become more aware of their responsibilities and their opportunities for furthering the mission of the church. The must not passively wait for directives or even an invitation from the clergy. As the Second Vatican Council has pointed out:

"Certain forms of the apostolate of the laity are given explicit recognition by the hierarchy, though in various ways. . . .

"Thus, making various dispositions of the apostolate according to circumstances, the hierarchy joins some particular form of it more closely with its own apostolic function. Yet the proper nature and individuality of each apostolate must be preserved, and the laity must not be deprived of the possibility of acting on their own accord."[17]

---

16. *Apostolicam Actuositatem* (Decree on the Apostolate of the Laity), 3.
17. *Ibid.*, 24.

Adulthood in Christ, to which all the laity are called, means seizing the opportunity for initiative and creativity in place of complaining about what cannot be done.

Above all, let there be no strife or conflict among us as a community and a people. How important it is to recognize and to respect each other's gifts! The pressures of the present age and the pressures of a minority status inevitably lead at times to self-doubt and even self-disdain. But there is always the love of Christ, which calls us beyond ourselves and even beyond our local concerns and rivalries.

"Each of us has received God's favor in the measure in which Christ bestows it. . . . It is he who gave apostles, prophets, evangelists, pastors and teachers in roles of service for the faithful to build up the body of Christ, till we become one in the faith and in the knowledge of God's Son, and form that perfect man who is Christ come to full stature" (Eph. 4:76, 11-13).

Youth

(Cf. "Evangelii Nuntiandi," 72.)

Our youth are the present and the future of the church in the Black community. If they must be the subject of evangelization in a special way, they should also be taught that they too have a unique opportunity to evangelize their peers.

Black youth are especially vulnerable in our modern society. Today's youth in the Black community undergo many pressures. Especially in our urban areas—where disillusionment and despair, desires and drugs, passion and poverty entrap the young—adults and mature youths dedicated to Christ are needed to counsel, to inspire and to motivate those whom Jesus loved and placed first in his kingdom. These youths in turn will be the heralds of the kingdom to other young people in our urban areas today.

Programs for youth—such as retreats, camps, recreational facilities, youth centers and vacation schools—need to be tailored for the Black community following the guidelines for youth ministry set up by the local church. Black Catholics who commit themselves to a vigorous youth ministry are to be commended and supported on the parish and diocesan level.

Rite of Christian Initiation of Adults

(Cf. "Evangelii Nuntiandi," 17-18, 23, 47.)

The newly restored Rite of Christian Initiation of Adults, creatively adapted to the life and culture of the Black community, will serve as a powerful instrument of evangelization among our people. The careful and thorough preparation of the catechumens; the appeal to the whole person, both head and heart (so characteristic of Black spirituality); the graduated liturgical stages of involvement by the whole Christian community—all these are features of the new rite which recommend it to us as especially useful for the work of evangelization.

We strongly urge that those among us competent to do so undertake as soon as possible the study needed to adapt the rite to the Black situation. We appeal to the appropriate authorities of the church to encourage this endeavor.

Catholic Education

(Cf. "Evangelii Nuntiandi," 40.)

Even prior to emancipation, Blacks in the United States clamored for educational opportunities. Families uprooted themselves, necessities were sacrificed, extra toil was assumed in order that the children would receive an education and, where possible, an even better one was expected for each succeeding child. Today many parents, very often single parents, make similar sacrifices; for Black people believe that the key to a better life is the school.

Black Catholics have placed their hope in Catholic schools with even greater zeal. The first Black Lay Catholic Congress in 1889 wrote:

"The education of a people being the great and fundamental means of elevating it to the higher planes to which all Christian civilization tends, we pledge ourselves to aid in establishing, wherever we are to be found, Catholic schools, embracing the primary and higher branches of knowledge, as in them and through them alone can we expect to reach the large masses of colored children now growing up in this country without a semblance of Christian education."[18]

Today the Catholic school still represents for many in the Black community, especially in the urban areas, an opportunity for quality education and character development. It also represents—and this is no less important—a sign of stability in an environment of chaos and flux. It should be a source of legitimate pride that our schools are sought after by many who are not Catholic as well as Catholics because of the religious and moral values considered as part of a quality education.

---

18. "Proceedings of the First Colored Catholic Congress Held in Washington, D.C., Jan. 1, 2 and 3, 1889," *Three Catholic Afro-American Congresses*, reprint ed. (New York, 1978), pp. 68-69.

The Catholic school has been and remains one of the chief vehicles of evangelization within the Black community. We cannot overemphasize the tremendous importance of parochial schools for the Black community. We even dare to suggest that the efforts made to support them and to ensure their continuation are a touchstone of the local church's sincerity in the evangelization of the Black community.

We are aware of the economic reality, but we are equally aware of the Gospel injunction to teach all peoples (cf. Mt. 28:19). Cost effectiveness can never be the sole criterion for decisions regarding the continuation of a Catholic school in the Black community. For this reason we express our profound admiration and deep gratitude to our fellow bishops, religious communities and laypersons, along with other church leaders who with a true evangelical spirit have done so much to maintain Catholic schools in our neighborhoods. We remind those who must make decisions concerning these schools to consult with the people of the community, inviting them to participate during the entire process when any decision concerning the existence of a particular school is to be made.

On the other hand, Catholic schools in our neighborhoods should be the concern of the entire Black community. As an important agent for evangelization they must be the concern even of those who have no children in the schools. By the same token, these schools must be thoroughly Catholic in identity and teaching. This does not mean coercing students to join the Catholic Church, but rather to expose all the students to the religious values and teaching that make these schools unique. In a particular way this means that faculty, administration, staff and students will by their manner of life bear witness to Gospel values. In this way not a few—as experience has shown—will freely choose to investigate the Catholic faith and seek fellowship within the Catholic community.

"All people should be able to recognize themselves when Christ is presented, and all should be able to recognize their own fulfillment when these mysteries are celebrated."

Support should also be given to Catholic and public institutions of higher learning as well as the traditional Black colleges which have particularly close ties with the Black community. Their excellence in scholarship and their continued growth should be a constant concern for Black Catholics. Xavier University in New Orleans, the only Black Catholic university in the United States, should hold a pride of place for us. Similarly, Newman centers on public campuses, which have the means of addressing the spiritual needs of our people, deserve our special attention.

Finally, we address an invitation to Black youth and Black adults to consider well the profession of teaching on all levels of Catholic education in our community. Theirs is a wonderful opportunity to spread the kingdom in the Black community.

"When a man is wise to his own advantage, the fruits of his knowledge are seen in his own person; when a man is wise to his people's advantage, the fruits of his knowledge are enduring" (Sir. 37:21-22).

Liturgy

(Cf. "Evangelii Nuntiandi," 17, 23, 42-43, 47.)

The celebration of the sacred mysteries is that moment when the church is most fully actualized and most clearly revealed. No treatment of evangelization would be complete without a discussion of the role of liturgy in this regard.

In the African-American tradition the communal experience of worship has always had a central position. In our heritage the moment of celebration has always been a time for praise and thanksgiving, and the affirmation of ourselves as God's children. It is a moment of profound expression, not a flight from reality (as some have suggested), but an experience of God's power and love.

From the standpoint of evangelization in the Black community, the liturgy of the Catholic Church has always demonstrated a way of drawing many to the faith and also of nourishing and deepening the faith of those who already believe. We believe that the liturgy of the Catholic Church can be an even more intense expression of the spiritual vitality of those who are of African origin, just as it has been for other ethnic and cultural groups:

"The church has no wish to impose a rigid uniformity in matters which do not involve the faith or the good of the whole community. Rather she respects and fosters the spiritual adornments and gifts of the various races and peoples."[19]

Through the liturgy, Black people will come to realize that the Catholic Church is a homeland for Black believers just as she is for people of other cultural and ethnic traditions. In recent years remarkable progress has been made in our country by many talented Black experts to adapt the liturgy to the needs and the genius of the African-American community. In order that this work can be carried on more fully within the Catholic tradition and at the same time be enriched by our own cultural heritage, we wish to recall the essential qualities that should be found in a liturgical celebration within the Black Catholic community. It should be authentically Black. It should be truly Catholic. And it should be well prepared and well executed.

Authentically Black: The liturgy is simultaneously a ritualization of the divine reality which transcends all human limitations and also and expression of what is more intimate and personal in

---

19. *Sacrosanctum Concilium* (Constitution on the Sacred Liturgy), 37.

the participants. What is expressed is the mystery of Christ, which transcends all cultures. The way, however, in which this mystery is expressed is mediated by the culture and traditions of the participants. All people should be able to recognize themselves when Christ is presented, and all should be able to experience their own fulfillment when these mysteries are celebrated. Hence, we can legitimately speak of an African-American cultural idiom or style in music, in preaching, in bodily expression, in artistic furnishings and vestments, and even in tempo. It is for this reason that we encourage those in pastoral ministry to introduce the African-American idiom into the expression of the Roman liturgy.

It is not our purpose at this time to detail all the characteristics this African-American cultural idiom may have nor to suggest the limits of cultural authenticity. It is important that from our own community there arise competent liturgical scholars and artists who will mutually contribute to a Black Catholic liturgical critique.

We do wish to remind our fellow Black Catholics, however, that the African-American cultural heritage is vast and rich. The cultural idiom of American Black people has never been uniform, but has varied according to region and ethos. African, Haitian, Latin and West Indian cultural expressions also continue to this day to nurture the Black American cultural expression. For this reason, an authentic Black Catholic liturgy need never be confined to a narrowly based concept of what is truly Black. There is a splendid opportunity for the vast richness of African-American culture to be expressed in our liturgy. It is this opportunity, thanks to the norms established in the revised Roman liturgy, which enables our work of evangelization to be filled with such promise for the future.

Truly Catholic: The liturgy not only expresses the worship of a given Catholic community, it also expresses the unity of the Catholic Church. Black Catholic liturgy should express not only our African-American cultural heritage, but also our Catholic faith and unity. In this way, unlike some other Christian communities in the Black community, our worship is not confined to preaching the word alone, but also includes the sacrament as celebration.

For this reason neither the preaching nor the music nor any other ritual action has exclusive domain at liturgical celebration. If one or the other prevails, the evangelical dimension as well as the prayerful experience of the liturgy suffers.

"Evangelization thus exercises its full capacity when it achieves the most intimate relationship, or better still, a permanent and unbroken intercommunication, between the word and the sacraments. In a certain sense it is a mistake to make a contrast between evangelization and sacramentalization. . . . The role of evangelization is precisely to educate people in the faith in such a way as to lead each individual Christian to live the sacraments as true sacraments of faith—and not to receive them passively or reluctantly."[20]

Both the liturgical preaching and the music should invite the worshiping community to a more profound participation in the total sacramental experience. Neither preaching nor music should overwhelm the liturgical worship and prevent it from exhibiting a balanced unified action.

Proper Preparation and Excellence in Execution: We wish to commend those who have tirelessly presented workshops and conferences on Black liturgical expression. We urge the continued training of liturgists and musicians from the Black Catholic community. We likewise wish to commend those who have generously given their talents as musicians and vocalists to continue to dedicate their skills in God's service. Finally, we urge men and women steeped in the African-American tradition and culture to collaborate with our liturgical scholars in the development of liturgical worship in our community. It is especially in this regard that we can use our rich gifts of blackness for the whole church.

In the liturgy, preparation begins with prayerful reflection and is completed and perfected by an execution that culminates in total prayer. We urge that this prayerful preparation and prayerful performance and execution be the result of a collaborative effort of many gifted people each Sunday in our parishes.

The Social Apostolate

(Cf. "Evangelii Nuntiandi," 8-12, 29-39.)

The proclamation of the good news by Jesus began with the proclamation of justice and compassion in the context of social reform:

"When the book of the prophet Isaiah was handed him, he unrolled the scroll and found the passage where it was written: 'The spirit of the Lord is upon me; therefore he has anointed me. He has sent me to bring glad tidings to the poor, to proclaim liberty to captives, recovery of sight to the blind and release to prisoners, to announce a year of favor from the Lord'' (Lk. 4:17-19).

For us the causes of justice and social concern are an essential part of evangelization. Our own history has taught us that preaching to the poor and to those who suffer injustice without concern for their plight and the systemic cause of their plight is to trivialize the Gospel and mock the cross. To preach to the powerful

---

20. "On Evangelization in the Modern World,' 47.

without denouncing oppression is to promise Easter without Calvary, forgiveness without conversion and healing without cleansing the wound.

Our concern for social justice, moreover, goes beyond denouncing injustice in the world around us. It brings us to the examination of our own hearts and intentions. It reminds us that it was the despised and rejected Samaritan who had the compassion to bind up the wounds of the other and to provide a lesson for the chosen (cf. Lk. 10:29-37). As Black people in a powerful nation we must have concern for those who hunger and thirst for justice everywhere in the present world. We must not forget that in a world of suffering even compassion may still be selective. Let us not ignore those whom others tend to forget. It should be our concern to remind others of the plight of Haitian refugees, the hunger of drought-ridden Africans, the forgotten Blacks in a war-torn Namibia and the many other forgotten minorities and ill-starred majorities in the world of the downtrodden and deprived. Political expediency and diplomatic advantages should not be brought with the human rights of others.

As a people we must have the courage to speak out and even contribute our efforts and money on behalf of any people or any segment of the human family that the powerful may seek to neglect or forget as a matter of policy. Be assured that we too must render an account for what the Lord has given us (cf. Ps. 116:12). When we share our talents and our possessions with the forgotten ones of this world, we share Christ. This is not the prelude to evangelization, it is the essence of evangelization itself.

CONCLUSION

(Cf. "Evangelii Nuntiandi," 3-4, 41-46, 68-69, 70-73, 78-79.)

We write this letter to you, our brothers and sisters, strong in the faith and in the knowledge that what has been begun in you will be brought to perfection in the day of our Lord Jesus Christ. We urge you to study and discuss the points laid before you in this, our pastoral letter. We ask that you heed the opportunities that are ours today. Let us not deprive the church of the rich gifts that God has granted us.

For this reason we write to you, brothers and sisters, in the many parishes across our country. We urge the Black people of these parishes to take to heart our words of encouragement to spread the message of Christ to our own and to those of all ethnic and racial groups. We ask pastors, co-pastors, pastoral assistants, classroom teachers and directors of religious education—indeed all who are staff and board members in the parish and in the diocese—to speak the good news clearly in the idiom and expression of our people. Let it be the responsibility every parish council and every parish team to ponder the meaning of Black evangelization and the burden of this pastoral letter in each respective community.

We write to those among us who are writers and poets, teachers and musicians, social scientists and theologians, philosophers and artists, academics and scholars—to all those who are the specialists whom we need to write the commentaries, edit the texts, lay out the critiques, analyze the possibilities, draw up the study guides and gather the bibliographies—to make our efforts for Black evangelization bear fruit in practical planning and innovative, imaginative proposals.

We turn to those of you who are lay leaders in the Black Catholic community. In a particular way it will be your ministry to help implement the actions called for in this letter—some on the diocesan level, others on the national level. We address the National Association of Black Catholic Administrators, the National Office for Black Catholics and the National Black Lay Catholic Caucus. You, and those whom you represent, will be the key to unlock the doors of opportunities for a wider field of evangelization in our community.

We ask especially our brothers and sisters in the priesthood, the diaconate and the religious life, and our sisters in the consecrated life, as well as our seminarians, to aid us by your ministry to make actual in a concrete way what we have sought to set forth in guidelines and suggested proposals. We ask for your experience as Black men and women of God, for your zealous support and for your broad vision to give us counsel and to facilitate our common task in the service of our own people.

We look to those who are responsible on the diocesan level for the various offices and departments of education and evangelization, administrators, teachers, directors; we turn to seminary teachers and staff as well as leaders of formation; we ask all to study the proposals gathered here and to take to heart the concerns of the church among the Black members of Christ's body as set forth above.

Finally, we ask you, brothers in the episcopacy, upon whom weigh the cares of all the churches and to whom the seamless robe of Christ's unity has been entrusted—we ask you, our brother bishops, to look carefully at the needs of those Black Catholics who reside within your care. Without your guidance and support the wealth of Black giftedness risks being lost, the abundance of our opportunities risks being squandered.

Last of all, we turn to Mary, the mother of God and the mother of the African-American community. She is the poor woman and the bearer of the word, the first to believe and the first to proclaim the word. We entrust to her powerful intercession this work within the Black community.

May our Heavenly Father perfect us, his church, in faith and love, that we might be always and everywhere faithful witnesses to the power of the resurrection of our Lord Jesus Christ, through whom be all the honor and the glory in the Holy Spirit, now and forever. Amen.

COCU: REPORT OF THE COMMISSION ON RACISM, NOVEMBER, 1984

The Consultation on Church Union has reached a decisive moment in its life. Years of accumulated experiences in attempting to live our way toward union have strengthened the bond between the participating churches, established some degree of trust, and reached beyond discussions among official delegates to worship, fellowship and mission among members and congregations in a number of geographical and social settings. An emerging theological consensus is on the threshold of adoption. The concept of covenanting has generated excitement. Concrete proposals for a radically new life together on the way toward a truly catholic, evangelical, and reformed, uniting church have been developed for presentation and discussion. Significant progress has been made to integrate the church dividing issues of the "Alerts" into the theological consensus. That work must continue in new areas of the life of the Consultation related to the development of covenanting as the vehicle which carries the Consultation into the future.

The various steps on the way toward covenanting are themselves important indicators of the commitment of the Consultation to become an inclusive church. The process of covenanting offers the opportunity for the Consultation to exhibit its desire for inclusiveness as that process unfolds in its several dimensions. With this in mind the Executive Committee established the Commission on Racism in October, 1983 with the following mandate:

> The Commission needs, in our judgment to have its central work on the envisioning of a church "truly inclusive." Though this is probably encompassed in the phrase "truly catholic," it is also somewhat obscured by the traditional way in which catholicity is defined and expressed. Out of the human experience, particularly the pain of every oppression comes a pointed and urgent, insistence on a church "truly inclusive."

The Commission is not a "strategic or programmatic commission but one that addresses the church-dividing meaning of racism and other similar kinds of oppression and abuse in the human experience."

Toward that end the Commission on Racism, having held two meetings, has begun its work. The Commission perceives part of its responsibility in terms of the covenanting process to be that of responding to the reports of the Church Order, Theology, and Worship Commissions. Time constraints have not permitted the Commission on Racism to fulfill this aspect of its task. However a formal response from the Commission to the other commission will be forthcoming.

The Commission on Racism understands its role in broader terms than the monitoring function. It perceives its primary task to be that of helping to create and develop an ecclesiology of inclusiveness so that the covenanting process and uniting church will be institutionally and personally free of the racism which currently afflicts and continues to divide the churches. This commission has already begun to engage this task in the preparation and distribution of three papers on the nature of the inclusive church from various minority and majority perspectives. This commission will continue to develop a vision of the inclusive church.

While the Commission on Racism commends the efforts of the Theology to incorporate the "Alerts" into the main body of the *Quest* document, it recognizes that there were points at which their inclusion did not flow as smoothly as might have been desired. This commission understands that part of the difficulty of including racism as a theological and ecclesiological issue in a document such as *Quest* has to do with the way that theology has been traditionally conceived. Traditionally racism has not been viewed as a classical theological or ecclesiological category. Consequently its inclusion in the *Quest* document as a "new" theological issue is strained at points. Thus the Commission is of the opinion that it ought to participate in other theological forums, which though broader than COCU, will affect the theological reflection which will go on in the COCU churches. The Commission strongly believes that these other forums need the perceptions and insights of racial ethnics and others who are particularly sensitive to the justice issues. Racial ethnics and others are extremely resistant to being typed cast, or stereotyped, or having their area of expertise and concern narrowly defined by others. If minorities are capable of thinking theologically about racism, then they are also capable of theological reflection on other issues, which may or may not impact the thinking of the churches regarding racism. Thus the Commission plans to participate in the World Council of Churches Apostolic Faith Study. The significance of the larger context for COCU, particularly as we begin to reflect upon the faith together as covenanting churches, would indicate the importance of COCU's participation as a whole, as well as this Commission's involvement in the Apostolic Faith Study.

The Commission is also giving some thought to an event which will center around the issue of ethnicity as a theological (creational) category, from which implications can be drawn for the wider church.

The Commission has felt hampered in its work by the lack of participation from all aspects of COCU's life. Some COCU churches have not been represented in any of the commission meetings to date, and some of our observer churches who are participants in every other commission have not sent representatives to this commission. We would hope that those churches not presently participating in the work of this commission will understand that its work is just as vital to the life of the Consultation as that of the other commissions. We would also hope that the reasons for the lack of participation are only bureaucratic.